MILITARY
Quotations

STIRRING WORDS OF WAR AND PEACE

RAY HAMILTON

summersdale

MILITARY QUOTATIONS

Summersdale Publishers Ltd
46 West Street
Chichester
West Sussex
PO19 1RP
UK

www.summersdale.com

Printed and bound by CPI Group (UK) Ltd, Croydon CR0 4YY

ISBN: 978-1-84953-327-0

Substantial discounts on bulk quantities of Summersdale books are available to corporations, professional associations and other organisations. For details telephone Nicky Douglas on (+44-1243-756902), fax (+44-1243-786300) or email (nicky@summersdale.com).

Contents

Acknowledgements

I am indebted to all the friends and family members who pointed me in the direction of a great quotation or story, and in particular to Ateesh Sidhu, Anthony Savell and my wife, Karen, for their many invaluable suggestions. I am grateful to Abbie Headon and Debbie Chapman at Summersdale, who have been a delight to work with, as always, and to Jennifer Barclay for enlisting me into the Summersdale ranks in the first place.

And, most of all, I owe Karen an enormous debt for kick-starting my hugely enjoyable second career.

Introduction

In searching for the quotations and stories that make up this book, I have travelled back and forward across continents and through the ages of time. I have poked my nose into dynasties, empires, republics and kingdoms, where I have encountered leaders, heroes, heroines, revolutionaries, warmongers, dictators, despots, diplomats, kings and queens, politicians, zealots and pacifists. I have observed the observers of history: the authors, poets, playwrights, philosophers, journalists, critics, historians, theologians and scientists – and pretty much anyone else who has had something to say about war or peace.

I have met a lot of old friends along the way. Memories of 'Stonewall' Jackson came flooding back when I was reminded of the American Civil War stories I studied in preparation for my History O Level exam. I bumped into the cowboys and Indians of my childhood; I saw again the Zulus and soldiers and gladiators and naval heroes who filled the silver screen of my most impressionable years. I even learned a lot of new stuff about those old friends, never having appreciated before that 'Stonewall' Jackson constantly fretted about having one arm shorter than the other, or that 'Che' Guevara did a stint down in the Congo, or that Napoleon might have been killed by his own wallpaper.

I have made a lot of new acquaintances as well, including a female Russian sniper who proved herself to be far more deadly than the male species around her, the first man to fly an aeroplane with no view outside the cockpit, the Maroons who camouflaged themselves as trees in order to slit the throats of the British soldiers who leaned against them to take a well-earned rest, the supermodel-turned-front-line war reporter who took a bath in Hitler's own tub, and Romania's own Joan of Arc.

I have also been reminded of stories that I have heard first-hand over the years. Bert England, our next-door neighbour in London for ten years, used to tell of the Mulberry pontoons he helped to build for the D-Day beach landings. Harold Bidwell, who used to live across the road from where we live now, remembered all too well the horrors of the World War Two jungles. And my late stepfather, 'Fred' De Marco, would regale the family with stories of his time serving with Montgomery's 'Desert Rats' in North Africa. My all-time favourite was his story about Corporal Jenkins, one of the cooks who was frying up breakfast one morning in early 1943 when German aircraft appeared from nowhere and opened fire over the Eighth Army's camp. Almost immediately, Jenkins fell to the ground, crying 'I've been hit'. And he had been – by his own sizzling hot sausages. They weren't even Frankfurters, which would at least have made them enemy sausages. The despatches for that particular day included the following entry:

Corporal Jenkins. Wounded by sausage.

I hope you enjoy reading the quotations and stories in this book half as much as I have enjoyed pulling them together. I am confident that there is something in here for everyone. I have tried to be unbiased in my selections, and I have not left out the authors who just got it all wrong, like the guys at *Time* magazine, who, in their 12 June 1939 edition, declared the French army to be 'still the strongest all-around fighting machine in Europe'. The French, incidentally, seem to get more than their fair share of stick when it comes to history, but if you're French and you want to get your own back, go straight to 'J' and enjoy the wounding rhetoric aimed back at the English by your very own Jeanne d'Arc.

Feel free to dip in and out to find your favourite leaders, heroes or poets, but read cover to cover if you don't want to miss the less well-known or anonymous quotations, like the following entry from a 1930s Soviet infantry manual:

> *Do not touch anything unnecessarily. Beware of pretty girls in dance halls and parks, who may be spies, as well as bicycles, revolvers, uniforms, arms, dead horses, and men lying on roads – they are not there accidentally.*

A

JOHN ADAMS

> We're in a war damn it, let's try
> to have an effect on that.

> I must study politics and war ... that my sons may
> have liberty to study mathematics and philosophy.

> Great is the guilt of an unnecessary war.

> In war, truth is the first casualty.

> I think the state care little a thing one or two arches

A

JOHN ADAMS

(1735–1826, SECOND PRESIDENT OF THE UNITED STATES)

We're in a war, dammit! We're going
to have to offend somebody!
*On becoming exasperated during the drafting
of the Declaration of Independence*

I must study politics and war, that our sons may
have liberty to study mathematics and philosophy.

Great is the guilt of an unnecessary war.

AESCHYLUS

(C. 525–456 BC, GREEK PLAYWRIGHT)

In war, truth is the first casualty.

I think the slain care little if they sleep or rise again.

AESOP

(C. 620–564 BC, GREEK STORYTELLER)

The shaft of the arrow had been feathered
with one of the eagle's own plumes. 'Alas,' it
cried, as it died, 'We often give our enemies
the means for our own destruction.'

Any excuse will serve a tyrant.

AGIS II

(DIED C. 401 BC, KING OF SPARTA)

The Spartans do not ask how many the
enemies are but where they are.

ANDREW AGNEW

(1687–1771, BRITISH ARMY COMMANDER)

Don't fire until you can see the whites of their eyes!

*Addressed to the 21st Foot of the Royal Scots Fusiliers as they
prepared to repel a French cavalry attack at Flanders in 1743*

ALEXANDER III OF MACEDON

(ALEXANDER THE GREAT) (356–323 BC, KING OF MACEDON)

I do not steal victory.

I am not afraid of an army of lions led by a sheep;
I am afraid of an army of sheep led by a lion.

ALWAYS MAKE SURE YOU GET YOUR FULL EIGHT HOURS' SLEEP BEFORE A BIG BATTLE

THE BATTLE OF GAUGAMELA, in modern-day Iraq, was fought in 331 BC between the Macedonian army of Alexander the Great and the Persian army of Darius III. Given that the Macedonians were seriously outnumbered, Alexander's generals tried to convince him on the eve of battle to attack during the night, thereby gaining the advantage of surprise. Alexander replied that he would not steal victory in such a way and ordered his men to get a good night's sleep. Alexander himself slept so well that his generals had to wake him up the next morning. Darius, on the other hand, fearing the nocturnal attack that never came, kept his army on high alert throughout the night.

The battle ended in a decisive victory for Alexander and heralded the end of the Persian Empire. It is widely accepted that Alexander's tactics were superior on the day, and that his army was better trained than that of Darius, but I like to think that the victory had more to do with the benefits of a good night's sleep!

ARNAUD AMALRIC

(DIED 1225, ABBOT OF CÎTEAUX)

Kill them all and let God sort them out.

At the Massacre of Béziers in 1209

PRINCE ANDREW

(BORN 1960, DUKE OF YORK)

When the question arose whether I as a member
of the royal family should take part in active
combat in the Falklands, there was no question
in her mind, though there was in other people's,
and it only took her two days to sort the issue.

*On the Queen's decision that he should serve in the
Falklands as a Royal Navy helicopter pilot*

ANONYMOUS

AIM towards the enemy.

Instruction printed on American rocket launcher

Chief among the spoils of victory is the
privilege of writing the history.

Do not touch anything unnecessarily. Beware
of pretty girls in dance halls and parks, who
may be spies, as well as bicycles, revolvers,
uniforms, arms, dead horses, and men lying
on roads – they are not there accidentally.

From Soviet infantry manual, 1930s

Friends, how much finer it is to die victorious in the
battle-line than to win at the Olympic games and live!

*A Spartan mother, upon hearing of her son's success in
battle, and of his death from his many wounds*

If God had meant for us to be in the army, we
would have been born with green, baggy skin.

It'll be a great day when education gets all
the money it wants and the Air Force has
to hold a bake sale to buy bombers.

Service conditions being what they are
today, a girl who marries an officer and a
gentleman usually has to commit bigamy.

American soldier, c. 1960

War is terrorism – with a bigger budget.

YASSER ARAFAT

(1929–2004, PALESTINIAN LEADER)

I come bearing an olive branch in one hand,
and the freedom fighter's gun in the other. Do
not let the olive branch fall from my hand.

Choose your friends carefully. Your
enemies will choose you.

ARCHIDAMUS II

(DIED 427 BC, KING OF SPARTA)

It is the noblest and safest thing for a great
army to be visibly animated by one spirit.

If we begin the war in haste, we'll have many delays
before we end it, owing to our lack of preparation.

ARISTOTLE

(384–322 BC, GREEK PHILOSOPHER)

We make war that we may live in peace.

Is there a more terrible scourge than
injustice with arms in its hands?

YAA ASANTEWAA

(1840–1921, ASHANTI QUEEN MOTHER)

If you, the men of Ashanti, will not go forward,
then we will. We, the women, will. I shall call upon
my fellow women. We will fight the white men. We
will fight till the last of us falls in the battlefields.

*Rising up against the British colonialists in 1900 when the male
tribal leaders appeared to lack the stomach for rebellion*

HERBERT HENRY ASQUITH

(1852–1928, BRITISH PRIME MINISTER)

If I am asked what we are fighting for, I can reply
in two sentences. In the first place, to fulfil a solemn
international obligation… an obligation of honour
which no self-respecting man could possibly have
repudiated. I say, secondly, we are fighting to vindicate
the principle that small nationalities are not to be
crushed in defiance of international good faith at the
arbitrary will of a strong and overmastering Power.

*Declaration of war against Germany in the
House of Commons in August 1914*

The War Office kept three sets of figures – one to mislead the public, another to mislead the Cabinet and the third to mislead itself.

The army will hear nothing of politics from me, and in return I expect to hear nothing of politics from the army.

MUSTAFA KEMAL ATATÜRK

(1881–1938, FIRST PRESIDENT OF TURKEY)

We must never say: 'What does it matter to me if some part of the world is ailing?' If there is such an illness, we must concern ourselves with it as though we were having that illness.

No inch of the motherland may be abandoned without being soaked in the blood of her sons.

ATHENAGORAS OF SYRACUSE

(FIFTH CENTURY BC, POLITICIAN)

If a man does not strike first, he will be the first struck.

MARCUS AURELIUS

(AD 121–180, ROMAN EMPEROR)

The secret of all victory lies in the organisation of the non-obvious.

B

Newton D. Baker

(1871–1937, US Secretary of War)

That idea is so damned nonsensical and impossible
that I'm willing to stand on the bridge of a battleship
while that nitwit tries to hit it from the air.

*Upon considering General Billy Mitchell's idea of using
aeroplanes to sink a battleship. In July 1921 Mitchell got
his experiment and sunk the captured German battleship
SMS Ostfriesland. Newton was not on the bridge.*

Stanley Baldwin

(1867–1947, three times British prime minister)

Since the day of the air, the old frontiers are gone.
When you think of the defence of England you no
longer think of the chalk cliffs of Dover; you think
of the Rhine. That is where our frontier lies.

House of Commons, July 1934

War would end if the dead could return.

FRANCESCO BARACCA

(1888–1918, ITALIAN WORLD WAR ONE FLYING ACE)

To the aircraft I aim, not the man.

PEDRO CALDERÓN DE LA BARCA

(1600–1681, SPANISH PLAYWRIGHT)

One may know how to gain a victory,
and know not how to use it.

CLARA BARTON

(1821–1912, AMERICAN CIVIL WAR UNION
NURSE AND HUMAN RIGHTS ACTIVIST)

I may be compelled to face danger, but never
fear it, and while our soldiers can stand and
fight, I can stand and feed and nurse them.

This conflict is one thing I've been waiting for. I'm
well and strong and young – young enough to go to
the front. If I can't be a soldier, I'll help soldiers.

FRANCK BAUER

(BORN 1919, FRENCH RADIO PRESENTER)

Ici Londres! Les français parlent aux français. (Here
is London. The French are speaking to the French.)

*Opening of broadcasts from London to France
by the Free French Forces from 1940 to 1944.
Franck Bauer was one of their spokesmen.*

ETHEL LYNN BEERS

(1827–1879, AMERICAN POET)

'All quiet along the Potomac,' they say,
'Except now and then a stray picket
Is shot, as he walks on his beat, to and fro,
By a rifleman hid in the thicket.'

*From the American Civil War poem 'All
Quiet Along the Potomac Tonight'*

HAROLD BEGBIE

(1871–1929, ENGLISH WRITER)

When the ships come back from slaughter,
and the troops march home from war;
When the havoc strewn behind us
threats the road that lies before,
Every hero shall be welcomed,
every orphan shall be fed,
By the man who stuck to business, by
the man who kept his head.

From the World War One poem 'The Man Who Keeps His Head'

How will you fare, sonny, how will you fare
In the far-off winter night,
When you sit by the fire in an old man's chair
And your neighbours talk of the fight?
Will you slink away, as it were from a blow,
Your old head shamed and bent?
Or say – I was not with the first to go,
But I went, thank God, I went?

*From the World War One poem 'Fall In',
addressed to conscientious objectors*

JANET BEGBIE

(BRITISH WORLD WAR ONE POET)

Carry on, carry on, for the men and boys are gone,
But the furrow shan't lie fallow
while the women carry on.

From the World War One poem 'Carry On'

IF THERE IS NO BREAD, LET THEM EAT STRAWBERRIES, APPLES AND PEARS!

JANET BEGBIE'S WORDS HELD good at the time her book of poetry, *Morning Mist,* was published in 1916, and they were to hold good again just over thirty years later. Food rationing was introduced in Britain during both World Wars and the nation relied on its Land Girls to 'dig for victory' on both occasions. The girls helped grow apples, pears and strawberries in British soil, although more exotic fruit like bananas, oranges and peaches were out of the question. When the government first set up the Women's Land Army in 1916, under the recruitment slogan 'God Speed the Plough and the Woman Who Drives It', many chauvinistic farmers remained unwilling to accept the female labour that was on offer. But the recruitment drive paid off and within a year 260,000 women were working as farm labourers in support of the war effort.

JOHNSON BEHARRY

(BORN 1979, BRITISH CORPORAL)

Maybe I was brave, I don't know. At the time I was just doing the job, I didn't have time for other thoughts.

*Speaking of the actions in Iraq in 2004 that
earned him the Victoria Cross*

JELLO BIAFRA

(BORN 1958, AMERICAN MUSICIAN AND ENVIRONMENTALIST)

We need a new law that owners of SUVs are automatically in the military reserve. Then they can go get their own goddamn oil.

Quoted in The Guardian, 3 November 2007

SERGEY BIRYUZOV

(1904–1964, SOVIET ARMY COMMANDER)

Permit me, in the name of the Front Command, to present you with the keys to the Crimea.

To Marshal Vasilevski, May 1944

OTTO VON BISMARCK

(1815–1898, GERMAN CHANCELLOR)

The main thing is to make history, not to write it.

Be polite; write diplomatically; even in a declaration
of war one observes the rules of politeness.

Anyone who has ever looked into the glazed
eyes of a soldier dying on the battlefield
will think hard before starting a war.

An appeal to fear never finds an
echo in German hearts.

WILHELM BITTRICH

(1894–1979, GERMAN SS PANZERKORPS OBERGRUPPENFÜHRER)

In all my years as a soldier, I have
never seen me fight so hard.

*Commenting on the British paratroopers after
the Battle of Arnhem, September 1944*

BLACK ELK

(1863–1950, SIOUX WARRIOR AND MEDICINE MAN)

There can never be peace between nations
until there is first known that true peace
which is within the souls of men.

We were warriors at a time when
boys now are like girls.

BLACK HAWK

(1767–1838, SAUK LEADER AND WARRIOR)

Courage is not afraid to weep, and she is not afraid to
pray, even when she is not sure who she is praying to.

How smooth must be the language of the
whites, when they can make right look
like wrong, and wrong like right.

Black Hawk has fought for his countrymen,
the squaws and papooses, against white men,
who came year after year, to cheat them and
take away their lands. You know the cause
of our making war. It is known to all white
men. They ought to be ashamed of it.

*From his speech on surrendering at the end
of the Black Hawk War in 1832*

BLACK KETTLE

(C. 1803–1868, CHEYENNE CHIEF)

All I ask is that we have peace with the whites…
We have been travelling through a cloud. The
sky has been dark ever since the war began.

I once thought that I was the only man that
persevered to be the friend of the white man,
but since they have come and cleaned out our
lodges, horses, and everything else, it is hard
for me to believe the white man any more.

TONY BLAIR

(BORN 1953, BRITISH PRIME MINISTER)

As for those that carried out these attacks, there are no adequate words of condemnation. Their barbarism will stand as their shame for all eternity.

There is no meeting of minds, no point of understanding with such terror. Just a choice: defeat it or be defeated by it. And defeat it we must.

The two quotes above were spoken after the attacks on the twin towers of the World Trade Centre in September 2001

As so often before, on the courage and determination of British men and women serving our country the fate of many nations rest.

Address to the nation on the invasion of Iraq in March 2003

WILLIAM BLAKE

(1757–1827, ENGLISH POET)

Bring me my Bow of burning gold;
Bring me my Arrows of desire:
Bring me my Spear: O clouds unfold!
Bring me my Chariot of fire!

I will not cease from Mental Fight,
Nor shall my Sword sleep in my hand:
Till we have built Jerusalem,
In England's green & pleasant Land.

From William Blake's poem 'And did those feet in ancient time',
first published in 1808, set to music by Hubert Parry in 1916,
and rescored by Edward Elgar for very large orchestras in 1922

ENGLAND'S NATIONAL ANTHEM?

AT THE GROUND AND in the bars around Twickenham each year, at the time of the Army v. Navy Rugby Union match, you will hear William Blake's 'Jerusalem' being belted out as enthusiastically as 'Land of Hope and Glory', 'Rule Britannia' and 'God Save the Queen'. The military bands of our armed forces seem equally happy with them all as anthems, but there is more controversy than you might imagine over which of the songs should be England's national anthem ('God Save the Queen' is the national anthem of the United Kingdom, as opposed to just England). 'Jerusalem' is considered to be England's most popular patriotic song (it has been said that George V preferred it to 'God Save the King'), and questions have even been raised in parliament by sporting bodies about which anthem should be used. Parliamentary answers state that there is no official anthem, and that each sport must make its own unofficial decision. And that's official.

WILLIAM BLUM

(BORN 1933, AMERICAN WRITER)

A terrorist is someone who has a bomb,
but doesn't have an air force.

NAPOLEON BONAPARTE

(1769–1821, FRENCH MILITARY LEADER AND EMPEROR)

I die prematurely, murdered by the English
oligarchy and its hired assassin.

Extract from Napoleon's will

DEATH BY WALLPAPER?

THERE ARE MANY THEORIES about what lay behind the cryptic claim in Napoleon's will that the English assassinated him. The post-mortem had declared his cause of death to be a perforated stomach ulcer and no more was thought about it. At least, not until the 1960s.

A number of Napoleon's staff kept locks of his hair as souvenirs and they have been passed down the generations, sometimes coming up for sale at auctions. This has allowed modern forensic science techniques to be applied to the Emperor's hair, with the surprising result that it contains significant levels of arsenic. Historians now ponder over who might have administered the poison, but another theory has it that Napoleon might have inhaled too many poisonous vapours from the green colouring pigment that was used in the manufacture of wallpaper at the time. But the theory would only hold good if the wallpaper in Napoleon's house had been green. A plea went out on BBC radio in the 1980s to see if any listeners could throw light on the subject and, lo and behold, a woman in Norfolk had a scrapbook dating from the 1820s, which contained a scrap of wallpaper pilfered in 1823 from the room in which Napoleon had died. It was green. Case solved.

An army marches on its stomach.

Death is nothing, but to live defeated and inglorious is to die daily.

A soldier will fight long and hard
for a bit of coloured ribbon.

France has more need of me than
I have need of France.

I can no longer obey; I have tasted
command, and I cannot give it up.

I made all my generals out of mud.

The battlefield is a scene of constant chaos.
The winner will be the one who controls that
chaos, both his own and the enemies'.

It requires more courage to suffer than to die.

Soldiers generally win battles;
generals get credit for them.

Take time to deliberate, but when the time for
action has arrived, stop thinking and go in.

The first virtue in a soldier is endurance of
fatigue; courage is only the second virtue.

War is the business of barbarians.

When soldiers have been baptised in the fire of a
battlefield, they have all one rank in my eyes.

England is a nation of shopkeepers.

*First coined by Adam Smith in The Wealth of Nations
in 1776, but used by Napoleon to explain why England
was not a worthy opponent for the invincible French*

Has Wellington nothing to offer
me but these Amazons?

On observing the advance of the Gordon Highlanders

In war, moral considerations make up three-quarters
of the game: the relative balance of manpower
accounts only for the remaining quarter.

Never interrupt your enemy while he's
making a mistake, that is bad manners.

You must not fear death, my lads; defy him,
and you drive him into the enemy's ranks.

You must not fight too often with one enemy,
or you will teach him all your art of war.

If you start to take Vienna – take Vienna.

Impossible is a word to be found only
in the dictionary of fools.

A leader is a dealer in hope.

A man will fight harder for his
interests than for his rights.

A revolution is an idea that has found its bayonets.

The allies we gain by victory will turn against
us upon the bare whisper of our defeat.

L'audace, l'audace, toujours l'audace.
(Daring, daring, always daring.)

VANNA BONTA

(BORN 1958, AMERICAN WRITER AND ACTRESS)

Poverty and war have no excuse.

PIERRE BOSQUET

(1810–1861, FRENCH ARMY GENERAL)

It is magnificent, but it is not war; it is madness.
*On seeing the charge of the Light Brigade
at the Battle of Balaclava in 1854*

BOUDICA

(OR BOADICEA) (DIED C. AD 61, BRITISH WARRIOR QUEEN)

I am not fighting for my kingdom and
wealth now. I am fighting as an ordinary
person for my lost freedom, my bruised
body, and my outraged daughters.

If you weigh well the strength of the armies, and
the causes of the war, you will see that in this
battle you must conquer or die. This is a woman's
resolve; as for men, they may live and be slaves.

ELIZABETH BOWEN

(1899–1973, ANGLO-IRISH WRITER)

Raids are slightly constipating.
Referring to the Blitz

Everything is very quiet, the streets are never crowded,
and the people one dislikes are out of town.

Referring to living in London during World War Two

OMAR N. BRADLEY

(1893–1981, AMERICAN ARMY GENERAL)

We know more about war than we know about peace,
more about killing than we know about living.

The way to win an atomic war is to
make certain it never starts.

If we continue to develop our technology
without wisdom or prudence, our servant
may prove to be our executioner.

Wars can be prevented... and we who fail to
prevent them must share in the guilt for the dead.

ROBERT THE BRUCE

(1274–1329, KING OF SCOTLAND)

For it is not for glory we fight, nor riches,
nor honour, but for freedom alone, which
no good man loses but with his life.

From the Declaration of Arbroath, 1320

You have bled with Wallace. Now bleed with me.

*Addressed to the Scottish troops before the
Battle of Bannockburn in 1314*

A SPLITTING HEADACHE

ROBERT THE BRUCE HAD for years employed guerrilla tactics to great effect after he had taken over from William Wallace as leader of the Scottish nationalist forces. He was, therefore, ill prepared to fight a more traditional pitched battle at Bannockburn in 1314, and against a much larger English army at that. But, against all the odds, the Scots won in spectacular fashion, partly due to greater knowledge of the terrain, and partly due to a single incident that happened early on in the battle. One of the English knights, Henry de Bohun, in full armour and on his warhorse, noticed Bruce taking time out on his pony and armed with nothing but an axe. De Bohun decided to seize his chance for personal glory and charged straight at the vulnerable Scottish king. Bruce held his ground, stood up in his stirrups and cleaved the knight's head in two with his axe. This probably worked wonders for the morale of the Scottish troops.

The Battle of Bannockburn is commemorated in 'Flower of Scotland', the anthem that is always sung before the Scottish rugby team takes to the field. The Princess Royal, as patron of the Scottish Rugby Union, often joins in. I wonder what Henry de Bohun would make of that.

EDMUND BURKE

(1729–1797, ANGLO-IRISH STATESMAN AND WRITER)

The only thing necessary for the triumph of evil is for good men to do nothing.

When bad men combine, the good must associate; else they will fall, one by one, an unpitied sacrifice in a contemptible struggle.

I venture to say no war can be long carried on against the will of the people.

ROBERT BURNS

(1759–1796, SCOTTISH POET)

Man's inhumanity to man
Makes countless thousands mourn!
From 'Man Was Made to Mourn'

When wild war's deadly blast was blawn,
And gentle peace returning,
Wi' mony a sweet babe fatherless,
And mony a widow mourning;
I left the lines and tented field,
Where lang I'd been a lodger,
My humble knapsack a' my wealth,
A poor and honest sodger (soldier).
From 'The Soldier's Return'

Scots, wha hae wi' Wallace bled,
Scots, wham Bruce has aften led;
Welcome to your gory bed.
Or to victorie!
Now's the day, and now's the hour;
See the front o' battle lour:
See approach proud Edward's pow'r –
Chains and slaverie!
From 'Bruce's Address To His Army At Bannockburn'

GEORGE W. BUSH

(BORN 1946, FORTY-THIRD PRESIDENT OF THE UNITED STATES)

We are in a fight for our principles, and our
first responsibility is to live by them.

Freedom itself was attacked this morning by a
faceless coward, and freedom will be defended.

*After the September 2001 attack on the twin
towers of the World Trade Centre*

What our enemies have begun, we will finish.

*On the first anniversary of the attack on the
twin towers of the World Trade Centre*

BRETT BUTLER

(BORN 1958, AMERICAN ACTRESS)

Maybe that's why men declare war – because
they have a need to bleed on a regular basis.

Referring to men not having to deal with monthly menstrual cycles

C

JULIUS CAESAR

(100–44 BC, ROMAN GENERAL AND LEADER)

When the swords flash let no idea of love, piety,
or even the face of your fathers move you.

Beware of the leader, who strikes the war drum in
order to transfer the citizens into patriotic glow;
patriotism is indeed a double-sided sword. It makes
the blood so boldly, like it constricts the intellect.

Veni, vidi, vici. (I came, I saw, I conquered.)
Commenting in 47 BC on his short war with Pharnaces
II of Pontus (in modern-day Turkey)

In war, events of importance are
the result of trivial causes.

Alea iacta est. (The die has been cast.)
Upon crossing the Rubicon river

War gives the right of the conquerors to impose any conditions they please upon the vanquished.

CALGACUS

(FIRST CENTURY AD, CALEDONIAN CHIEFTAIN)

To theft, slaughter, and rapine they deceitfully name Empire; and even where they make a desert, they call it peace.

Said to his army before the Battle of Mons Graupius in AD 84

CALIGULA

(AD 12–41, ROMAN EMPEROR)

Let them hate as long as they fear.

PIERRE CAMBRONNE

(1770–1842, FRENCH GENERAL)

Merde!

When asked to surrender following the Battle of Waterloo

JIMMY CARTER

(BORN 1924, THIRTY-NINTH PRESIDENT OF THE UNITED STATES)

War may sometimes be a necessary evil. But no matter how necessary, it is always an evil, never a good. We will not learn how to live together in peace by killing each other's children.

FIDEL CASTRO

(BORN 1926, CUBAN PRESIDENT)

I am Fidel Castro and we have come to liberate Cuba.

I began the revolution with eighty-two men. If I had
to do it again, I would do it with ten or fifteen men
and absolute faith. It does not matter how small
you are if you have faith and a plan of action.

A revolution is a struggle to the death
between the future and the past.

LOUIS-FERDINAND CÉLINE

(1894–1961, FRENCH WRITER)

The poetry of heroism appeals irresistibly
to those who don't go to a war.

CHARLES II

(1630–1685, KING OF ENGLAND, SCOTLAND AND IRELAND)

It is upon the navy under the good Providence
of God that the safety, honour, and welfare
of this realm do chiefly depend.

In this wood I stayed all day without meat or drink
and by great fortune it rained all the time which
hindered them, as I believe, from coming into the
wood to search for men that might be fled there.

*Recounting the time he spent hiding from the
Roundheads after the Battle of Worcester*

I'LL SEE YOU UP 'THE ROYAL OAK' TONIGHT, BOYS

CHARLES II WAS UNABLE TO chiefly depend on the navy at the landlocked Battle of Worcester in 1651. It was the final battle of the English Civil War, at which the New Model Army of Oliver Cromwell overwhelmed his Royalist troops. Charles went on the run, a wanted man with a £1,000 bounty on his head. He made for the Boscobel estate, a Catholic stronghold with good hiding places (Catholics had become very good at hiding in Cromwell's time). There it was decided that he should spend the night up a large oak tree in the grounds.

Being 6 foot 2 inches tall and sporting a rather distinctive wig, he was not an easy man to hide up a tree, but heavy rain hampered the efforts of the Roundheads to find him and he would eventually make good his escape to France. Upon his return from exile when the monarchy was restored in 1660, the story of the oak tree became legend, immortalised in pottery and in vast numbers of pub signs. 'The Royal Oak' remains to this day one of the most popular pub names in England.

CHARLES XII

(1682–1718, SWEDISH KING)

I have resolved never to start an unjust
war, but never to end a legitimate one
except by defeating my enemies.

This shall hence become my music.

Upon hearing the sound of gunfire in his first battle

CHEESEEKAU

(OR CHIKSIKA) (1760–1792, SHAWNEE CHIEF)

When a white army battles Indians and
wins, it is called a great victory, but if
they lose it is called a massacre.

G. K. CHESTERTON

(1874–1936, ENGLISH WRITER)

The true soldier fights not because he hates what is in
front of him, but because he loves what is behind him.

The Bible tells us to love our neighbours, and
also to love our enemies; probably because
generally they are the same people.

JACQUES CHIRAC

(BORN 1932, FRENCH PRESIDENT)

Terrorism has become the systematic weapon of a war that knows no borders or seldom has a face.

National missile defence is of a nature to retrigger a proliferation of weapons, notably nuclear missiles. Everything that goes in the direction of proliferation is a bad direction.

AGATHA CHRISTIE

(1890–1976, ENGLISH WRITER)

[One has] the horrible feeling now that war settles nothing; that to win a war is as disastrous as to lose one.

WINSTON CHURCHILL

(1874–1965, BRITISH PRIME MINISTER AND WAR LEADER)

We shall defend our island, whatever the cost may be; we shall fight on the beaches, we shall fight on the landing grounds, we shall fight in the fields and in the streets, we shall fight in the hills; we shall never surrender.

Never in the field of human conflict was so much owed by so many to so few.

Referring in August 1940 to the RAF pilots who were at the time fighting the Battle of Britain against the German Luftwaffe

May it not also be that the cause of civilisation itself
will be defended by the skill and devotion of a few
thousand airmen? There never has been, I suppose,
in all the world, in all the history of war, such an
opportunity for youth. The Knights of the Round
Table, the Crusaders, all fall back into the past.

It is not good enough that we do our best.
Sometimes we have to do what is required.

I have never accepted what many people have
kindly said, namely that I inspired the nation.
It was the nation and the race dwelling around
the globe that had the lion heart. I had the
luck to be called upon to give the roar.

I would say to the House, as I said to those who
have joined this Government: 'I have nothing
to offer but blood, toil, tears, and sweat.'

We will have no truce or parley with you, or
the grisly gang who do your wicked will. You
do your worst – and we will do our best.
Directed at Adolf Hitler

In war, resolution; in defeat, defiance; in
victory, magnanimity; in peace, goodwill.

Nothing is so exhilarating in life as
to be shot at with no result.

'Not in vain' may be the pride of those who
survived and the epitaph of those who fell.
Speaking in the House of Commons in 1944
following the Battle of Arnhem

To the ferocity of the Zulu are added the craft of
the Redskin and the marksmanship of the Boer.

*Referring to the Pashtun tribesmen he had
encountered in 1897 in the Swat valley*

NINETEENTH-CENTURY CHURCHILL

GIVEN THE HUGE PART that Churchill played in
shaping the twentieth century, it is easy to forget
that he had already enjoyed a busy and incident-
packed twenty-six years before he even reached
the century that he was to have such enormous
influence over.

Having spent long enough as a military observer
in Cuba to be shot at by guerrillas on his twenty-
first birthday, and to develop a taste for fat Havana
cigars, the young Winston Churchill travelled as
a war reporter in 1897 to the Swat valley of the
North West Frontier, on what is now the still-
troubled Afghan-Pakistan border but which was
then part of British India. He was attached to the
Malakand Field Force, the British expeditionary
force that had been dispatched to put down the
rebellious tribesmen of the region. Having come
under fire when his patrol was ambushed, he later
wrote that the British were at a severe disadvantage
when faced with the fierce warriors of the Pashtun
tribes, who, armed with long-handled muskets,
were able to shoot and kill from an impressively
long distance and then disappear. He still had time
to see action under Lord Kitchener in the Sudan
and travel to South Africa in time for the start
of the Second Boer War by the turn of the new
century. He had started his life as he meant to go
on – at full speed ahead.

Dictators ride to and fro upon tigers, which they dare
not dismount. And the tigers are getting hungry.

I admire men who stand up for their country in
defeat, even though I am on the other side.

If you're going through hell, keep going.

Let us therefore brace ourselves to our duties,
and so bear ourselves that, if the British Empire
and its Commonwealth last for a thousand years,
men will still say, 'This was their finest hour.'
June 1940

One day President Roosevelt told me that he was
asking publicly for suggestions about what the war
should be called. I said at once 'The Unnecessary War'.

We have never been likely to get into trouble by having
an extra thousand or two up-to-date aeroplanes at our
disposal. As the man whose mother-in-law had died in
Brazil replied, when asked how the remains should be
disposed of, 'Embalm, cremate, bury. Take no risks.'

Air power may either end war or end civilisation.
To the House of Commons, 14 March 1933

The fighters are our salvation but the bombers
alone provide the means of victory.
*Referring in 1940 to the airmen of Fighter
Command and Bomber Command*

I felt as if I were walking with destiny, and that all my past life had been but a preparation for this hour and for this trial… I thought I knew a good deal about it all, I was sure I should not fail.

Writing about his time as Britain's war leader

MARCUS TULLIUS CICERO

(106–43 BC, ROMAN STATESMAN AND PHILOSOPHER)

The sinews of war are infinite money.

An unjust peace is better than a just war.

During war, the laws are silent.

BLAKE CLARK

(BORN 1946, AMERICAN ACTOR, COMEDIAN AND VIETNAM WAR VETERAN)

Being in the army is like being in the Boy Scouts, except that the Boy Scouts have adult supervision.

CARL VON CLAUSEWITZ

(1780–1831, PRUSSIAN MAJOR GENERAL AND AUTHOR OF 'PRINCIPLES OF WAR', 1812)

If the leader is filled with high ambition and if he pursues his aims with audacity and strength of will, he will reach them in spite of all obstacles.

Politics is the womb in which war develops.

We shall not enter into any of the abstruse
definitions of war used by publicists. We shall
keep to the element of the thing itself, to a duel.
War is nothing but a duel on an extensive scale.

Close combat, man to man, is plainly to be
regarded as the real basis of combat.

Never forget that no military leader has
ever become great without audacity.

On no account should we overlook the moral
effect of a rapid, running assault. It hardens
the advancing soldier against danger, while the
stationary soldier loses his presence of mind.

The more a general is accustomed to place
heavy demands on his soldiers, the more
he can depend on their response.

GEORGES CLEMENCEAU

(1841–1929, FRENCH PRIME MINISTER)

A man who has to be convinced to act before he acts
is not a man of action. You must act as you breathe.

War is much too serious a matter to
be entrusted to the military.

War is a series of catastrophes that results in a victory.

The graveyards are full of indispensable men.

CLEOPATRA

(C. 69–30 BC, EGYPTIAN QUEEN)

I will not be triumphed over.

THE LEADING LADY THAT FAILED TO SHOW

IT WAS TRADITIONAL IN Ancient Rome for conquering heroes to put on lavish processions to display the spoils of their wars. Hordes of defeated troops would shuffle by in chains and the procession would have as its prize exhibit a defeated king or general, to be ritually humiliated and quite often executed in front of those who had queued all night to get the best places in the forum.

When Octavian returned in 29 BC to celebrate his victories over Mark Anthony and Cleopatra, his prize exhibit would undoubtedly have been Cleopatra herself, but the much-reported asp to the bosom was to deny him that particular avenue of pleasure. It is a moot point whether Cleopatra did in fact commit suicide in order 'not to be triumphed over', or whether the asp had been administered on Octavian's orders for fear that the humiliation and public execution of such a beautiful queen might be considered distasteful, even by Roman standards.

BILL CLINTON

(BORN 1946, FORTY-SECOND PRESIDENT OF THE UNITED STATES)

We must teach our children to resolve their conflicts with words, not weapons.

[The real differences around the world] are between those who embrace peace and those who would destroy it... between those who open their arms and those who are determined to clench their fists.

TIM COLLINS

(BORN 1960, BRITISH ARMY OFFICER)

If there are casualties of war then remember that when they woke up and got dressed in the morning they did not plan to die this day. Allow them dignity in death.

It is a big step to take another human life. It is not to be done lightly. I know of men who have taken life needlessly in other conflicts. I can assure you they live with the mark of Cain upon them.

Excerpts from Tim Collins' inspirational eve-of-battle speech to the 1st Battalion, Royal Irish Regiment prior to the invasion of Iraq in 2003

CONFUCIUS

(551–479 BC, CHINESE POLITICIAN AND PHILOSOPHER)

To see the right and not to do it is cowardice.

To lead untrained people to war
is to throw them away.

Before you embark on a journey
of revenge, dig two graves.

WILLIAM CONGREVE
(1670–1729, ENGLISH PLAYWRIGHT)

Fear comes from uncertainty. When we are
absolutely certain, whether of our worth or
worthlessness, we are almost impervious to fear.

CONSTANTINE
(THE GREAT) (C. AD 272–337, ROMAN EMPEROR)

In this sign (of the Cross) thou shalt conquer.
*Following his controversial conversion to Christianity in the
fourth century, being the first Roman emperor to do so*

NORMAN 'DUTCH' COTA
(1893–1971, AMERICAN ARMY MAJOR GENERAL)

Gentlemen, we are being killed on the
beaches. Let us go inland and be killed.
Omaha Beach, Normandy, June 1944

OLIVER CROMWELL

(1599–1658, ENGLISH SOLDIER AND STATESMAN)

A few honest men are better than numbers.

I had rather have a plain, russet-coated Captain that knows what he fights for, and loves what he knows, than what you call a Gentleman and is nothing else.

Not only strike while the iron is hot,
but make it hot by striking.

GEORGE ARMSTRONG CUSTER

(1839–1876, AMERICAN CAVALRY COMMANDER)

I appeal to you as a soldier to spare me the humiliation of seeing my regiment march to meet the enemy and I not share its dangers.

There are not enough Indians in the world
to defeat the Seventh Cavalry.

D

ROALD DAHL

(1916–1990, ENGLISH FLYING ACE AND WING COMMANDER)

The only way to conduct oneself in a situation
where bombs rained down and bullets
whizzed past, was to accept the dangers.

From his memoir Going Solo

BẢO ĐẠI

(1913–1997, LAST EMPEROR OF VIETNAM)

If your government had given me a thousandth of the
sum it spent to depose me, I could have won that war.

*Referring to the occupying French in what was
then Annam in French Indo-China*

NEVER FLY WITH A GREMLIN IN THE WORKS

ROALD DAHL JOINED THE RAF in Nairobi in 1939. He trained in a de Havilland Tiger Moth over Kenya and in a Gloster Gladiator, the last fighter biplane used by the RAF, over Iraq. He was hospitalised for a few months after crash-landing the Gladiator in the Libyan Desert but he returned in 1941 to fly Hawker Hurricanes in the Greek Campaign. He was credited with five kills (which is the requirement to go down in history as a 'flying ace'), including one when he single-handedly attacked six Junkers Ju 88s that he came across bombing ships in the Mediterranean.

Suffering from blackouts as a result of his earlier injuries, he was sent in 1942 as an Assistant Air Attaché to Washington, where he worked with the likes of C. S. Forester and Ian Fleming to promote the war effort and attempt to convince the Americans to join in. He submitted some RAF anecdotes for Forester to shape into a story for *The Saturday Evening Post*, but Forester used them exactly as they were and told Dahl, 'I haven't changed a thing. Did you know you could write?'

I wonder what ever became of Wing Commander Dahl? If only he had written a story about gremlins sabotaging Hawker Hurricanes in World War Two, children would have loved it!

I would prefer to be a citizen of an independent
country rather than Emperor of an enslaved one.

I do not wish a foreign army to spill
the blood of my people.

ÉDOUARD DALADIER

(1884–1970, FRENCH PRIME MINISTER)

If the blood of France and of Germany flows again,
as it did twenty-five years ago, in a longer and even
more murderous war, each of the two peoples will fight
with confidence in its own victory, but the most certain
victors will be the forces of destruction and barbarism.

Before the outbreak of World War Two

SALVADOR DALÍ

(1904–1989, SPANISH ARTIST)

Wars never hurt anybody except the people who die.

'DAN' DALY

(1873–1937, UNITED STATES MARINES)

Come on, you sons of bitches!
Do you want to live forever?

*Prior to attacking the Germans at the Battle
of Belleau Wood in World War One*

JOSEPHUS DANIELS

(1862–1948, US SECRETARY OF THE NAVY)

There is no rank in sacrifice.

Army: A body of men assembled to rectify
the mistakes of the diplomats.

Defeat never comes to any man until he admits it.

STEPHEN DECATUR

(1779–1820, AMERICAN NAVAL OFFICER)

It is part of a sailor's life to die well.

*On the death in 1813 of Captain James Lawrence
during the Anglo-American War*

DON DELILLO

(BORN 1936, AMERICAN WRITER)

It is interesting… how weapons
reflect the soul of the maker.

PIERRE DESPROGES

(1939–1988, FRENCH HUMORIST)

One mustn't despair of imbeciles. With a little bit
of training, we can make soldiers out of them.

CUT NYAK DHIEN

(1850–1908, ACEHNESE GUERRILLA LEADER)

As Acehnese women, we may not shed tears for
people who have become shahid (martyred).

*Remonstrating with her daughter for crying at the news that her
father, Cut Nyak Dhien's husband, had been killed in battle*

DIONYSIUS OF HALICARNASSUS

(C. 60–7 BC, GREEK HISTORIAN)

Only the brave enjoy noble and glorious deaths.

BENJAMIN DISRAELI

(1804–1881, BRITISH PRIME MINISTER)

The services in wartime are fit only for
desperadoes, but in peace are only fit for fools.

The difference of race is one of the reasons
why I fear war may always exist; because race
implies difference, difference implies superiority,
and superiority leads to predominance.

War is never a solution; it is an aggravation.

'JIMMY' DOOLITTLE

(1896–1993, AMERICAN AIR FORCE GENERAL)

There's nothing stronger than the heart of a volunteer.

HE COULDN'T TALK TO THE ANIMALS, BUT HE COULD FLY BLIND

GENERAL 'JIMMY' DOOLITTLE WAS an American aviation pioneer and much-decorated officer in the American air force. His active service included the command of the first retaliatory aerial attack on Japanese soil following the attack on Pearl Harbour. The attack was a success and he and his crew bailed out successfully over China after, as anticipated, they ran out of fuel. Chinese guerrillas helped them through Japanese lines to safety. Doolittle subsequently received the Medal of Honor from Franklin D. Roosevelt.

In between periods of active service, he amassed a number of air speed records and performed the first 'outside loop' – diving from a height of 10,000 feet, he reached 280 miles an hour before bottoming out upside down and climbing to complete the loop. This manoeuvre had previously been considered fatal.

He was also an excellent aeronautical technician and fearless test pilot. He combined the two sets of skills to develop instrument flying and, in 1929, to become the first pilot to take off, fly and land an aeroplane with no view outside the cockpit. These accomplishments ultimately made all-weather flights available to us all.

Given the many risks he faced, probably his greatest accomplishment was to die of old age at 96.

One purpose was to give the folks at home the
first good news that we'd had in World War Two.
It caused the Japanese to question their warlords.
And from a tactical point of view, it caused the
retention of aircraft in Japan for the defence of
the home islands when we had no intention of
hitting them again seriously in the near future.

*Speaking about his command of the first aerial attack on
Japanese soil following the attack on Pearl Harbour*

If we should have to fight, we should be prepared to do
battle from the neck up instead of from the neck down.

The first lesson is that you can't lose a
war if you have command of the air, and
you can't win a war if you haven't.

ABDUL RASHID DOSTUM

(BORN 1954, AFGHAN ARMY GENERAL)

I asked for a few Americans. They brought
with them the courage of a whole army.

On the arrival of the Green Berets in Afghanistan in 2001

STEPHEN A. DOUGLAS

(1813–1861, AMERICAN POLITICIAN)

There are only two sides to this question. Every man
must be for the United States or against it. There can
be no neutrals in this war; only patriots and traitors.

Speaking at the outbreak of the American Civil War

FREDERICK DOUGLASS

(1818–1895, AMERICAN REFORMER)

A battle lost or won is easily described,
understood, and appreciated, but the moral
growth of a great nation requires reflection,
as well as observation, to appreciate it.

GIULIO DOUHET

(1869–1930, ITALIAN ARMY GENERAL)

Victory smiles upon those who anticipate the
changes in the character of war, not upon those
who wait to adapt themselves after they occur.

MICHAEL DRAYTON

(1563–1631, ENGLISH POET)

Upon Saint Crispin's Day
Fought was this noble fray,
Which fame did not delay
To England to carry.
O when shall English men
With such acts fill a pen?
Or England breed again
Such a King Harry?

From his poem 'Agincourt'

E

ABBA EBAN

(1915–2002, ISRAELI DIPLOMAT)

History teaches us that men and nations only behave wisely once they have exhausted all other alternatives.

THOMAS EDISON

(1847–1931, AMERICAN INVENTOR)

Non-violence leads to the highest ethics, which is the goal of all evolution. Until we stop harming all other living beings, we are still savages.

There will one day spring from the brain of science a machine or force so fearful in its potentialities, so absolutely terrifying, that even man, the fighter, who will dare torture and death in order to inflict torture and death, will be appalled, and so abandon war forever.

ALBERT EINSTEIN

(1879–1955, GERMAN PHYSICIST)

The world is a dangerous place, not
because of those who do evil, but because
of those who look on and do nothing.

You cannot simultaneously prevent
and prepare for war.

NOBODY EVER SAID BEING A
GENIUS WOULD BE EASY

EINSTEIN WAS A COMMITTED pacifist from an early
age and only very reluctantly accepted that arms
might indeed be needed as a deterrent to the evils
of Nazi Germany. All his life he was torn between
the astonishing capabilities of applied physics and
the horrific uses to which politicians and military
leaders could put them. He was appalled by the
impact of the atomic bombs dropped on Japan
in 1945, and the first test of a hydrogen bomb
in 1952 did nothing to alleviate his fears for the
future of mankind. The explosion of the H-bomb
was found to have synthesised a new chemical
element and in 1955, the year of Einstein's death,
it was given a name – einsteinium. It is difficult to
think of a less appropriate memorial to a man who
proved the existence of atoms, helped demonstrate
their enormous power and then spent much of his
life trying to stop people turning that scientific
knowledge into weapons of mass destruction.

I do not know with what weapons World War
Three will be fought, but World War Four
will be fought with sticks and stones.

Nationalism is a childhood disease.
It's the measles of humanity.

The release of atom power has changed
everything except our way of thinking.

DWIGHT D. EISENHOWER

(1890–1969, THIRTY-FOURTH PRESIDENT OF THE UNITED STATES)

What counts is not necessarily the size of the dog
in the fight – it's the size of the fight in the dog.

Every gun that is made, every warship launched,
every rocket fired, signifies... a theft from those who
hunger and are not fed, those who are cold and are
not clothed. This world in arms is not spending money
alone. It is spending the sweat of its labourers, the
genius of its scientists, the hopes of its children.

You are about to embark upon the Great Crusade,
toward which we have striven these many months. The
eyes of the world are upon you. The hope and prayers
of liberty-loving people everywhere march with you.

The tide has turned! The free men of the
world are marching together to Victory!

*Two excerpts from Eisenhower's Order of the Day
message to the soldiers, sailors and airmen of the Allied
Expeditionary Force before the Normandy landings*

MY BAD!

What did not come to light until well after the Normandy landings was a second draft message that Eisenhower had prepared in the event that the D-Day landings proved unsuccessful:

Our landings in the Cherbourg-Havre area have failed to gain a satisfactory foothold and I have withdrawn the troops. My decision to attack at this time and place was based upon the best information available. The troops, the Air (Force) and Navy did all that bravery and devotion to duty could do. If any blame or fault attaches to the attempt, it is mine alone.

This note was directed to the world. In it, Eisenhower commended the courage and commitment of the troops who, he wrote, had done all they could, and put the blame for failure entirely at his own door. He could have shared the blame with the weather, with the fatigue of the troops, with the superior field positions of the Germans, with any number of things. But he didn't. And, as it turned out, he didn't need to.

T. S. ELIOT

(1888–1965, BRITISH-AMERICAN WRITER)

The Civil War is not ended: I question whether any serious civil war ever does end.

ELIZABETH I

(1533–1603, QUEEN OF ENGLAND AND IRELAND)

Monarchs ought to put to death the authors and instigators of war, as their sworn enemies and as dangers to their states.

Though the sex to which I belong is considered weak, you will nevertheless find me a rock that bends to no wind.

There is nothing about which I am more anxious than my country, and for its sake I am willing to die ten deaths, if that be possible.

I know I have the body but of a weak and feeble woman; but I have the heart and stomach of a king, and of a king of England, and think foul scorn that Parma or Spain, or any prince of Europe, should dare to invade the borders of my realm.

From her inspirational speech to the troops at Tilbury in 1588

IT WAS A GOOD SPEECH ANYWAY

IT IS OFTEN REPORTED that Elizabeth I delivered her most famous speech on the eve of the Spanish Armada attack, but in fact she went to Tilbury over two weeks after the Spanish galleons had first engaged the English Navy in the Channel. English ships were already chasing the Armada up the North Sea and the troops gathered at Tilbury were preparing to defend against a follow-up attack planned by the Duke of Parma from The Netherlands. The attack never happened, dogged by the same indecision and unfavourable winds that had scuppered the main armada invasion in the first place. The troops were stood down two days later but the speech worked wonders for the morale of the nation and for Elizabeth's standing as queen. The ensuing victory celebrations rivalled that of her coronation thirty years earlier and she would dine out for a long time on this evidence of her strong leadership.

ELIZABETH II

(BORN 1926, QUEEN OF THE UNITED KINGDOM AND OF THE COMMONWEALTH REALMS)

In remembering the appalling suffering of war on both sides, we recognise how precious is the peace we have built in Europe since 1945. It is difficult for someone of my generation to over-emphasise this.

Speaking in Berlin in 2004

We lost the American colonies because we lacked
the statesmanship to know the right time and the
manner of yielding what is impossible to keep.

*Speaking in Philadelphia in July 1976 during the
bicentennial celebrations of American Independence*

You're very special... It's been rather a long
time since I've awarded one of these.

In awarding the Victoria Cross to Johnson Beharry in 2005

We are trying to do all we can to help our
gallant sailors, soldiers and airmen, and we
are trying, too, to bear our own share of the
danger and sadness of war. We know, every
one of us, that in the end all will be well.

*The fourteen-year-old Princess Elizabeth making her first radio
broadcast in 1940, during the BBC's Children's Hour. She
was addressing the children who had been evacuated away
from the cities as well as those who had been sent abroad.*

HAVELOCK ELLIS

(1859–1939, ENGLISH PHYSICIAN, PSYCHOLOGIST AND WRITER)

There is nothing that war has ever achieved
that we could not better achieve without it.

ALICE THOMAS ELLIS

(1932–2005, BRITISH WRITER)

Men were made for war. Without it they wandered
greyly about, getting under the feet of the women.

Ralph Waldo Emerson

(1803–1882, American writer)

The characteristic of genuine heroism is its persistency. All men have wandering impulses, fits and starts of generosity. But when you have resolved to be great, abide by yourself, and do not weakly try to reconcile yourself with the world. The heroic cannot be common, nor the common heroic.

The real and lasting victories are those of peace, and not of war.

Desiderius Erasmus

(1466–1536, Dutch humanist)

The most disadvantageous peace is better than the most just war.

War is delightful to those who have had no experience of it.

Euripides

(c. 480–406 BC, Greek playwright)

Ten soldiers wisely led will beat a hundred without a head.

Danger gleams like sunshine to a brave man's eyes.

Courage may be taught as a child is taught to speak.

The God of War hates those who hesitate.

EDWARD EVERETT

(1794–1865, AMERICAN POLITICIAN)

Education is a better safeguard of
liberty than a standing army.

God bless the Union – it is dearer to us for the blood
of brave men which has been shed in its defence.

Let a nation's fervent thanks make some amends
for the toils and sufferings of those who survive.

JOHANN VON EWALD

(1744–1813, GERMAN-DANISH MILITARY OFFICER)

Demoralise the enemy, then annihilate them.

There is nothing impossible! Give your
orders, support them with firmness, and
you will see every obstacle vanish!

F

Julio León Fandiño

(EIGHTEENTH CENTURY, SPANISH NAVAL CAPTAIN)

Go and tell your King that I will do the
same, if he dares to do the same.

After cutting off the ear of Captain Robert Jenkins

David G. Farragut

(1801–1870, AMERICAN CIVIL WAR UNION NAVAL OFFICER)

Damn the torpedoes. Full speed ahead!

*After his leading ship was hit by a mine (then called
a torpedo) at the Battle of Mobile Bay in 1864*

AN EAR FOR AN EAR

IN 1731, AT A time when Anglo-Spanish relations were particularly strained, the Spanish coast guard, led by commander Julio León Fandiño, boarded the British brig Rebecca. Fandiño accused the British captain, Robert Jenkins, of piracy, and cut off his left ear. Fandiño then told him, 'Go and tell your King that I will do the same, if he dares to do the same.' In 1738, Jenkins was ordered to attend Parliament to tell his story to the House of Commons; legend has it that he even produced the severed ear, although there is no official record of his hearing at the time (at least not on his left side). Parliament considered the severed ear the worst insult in a long line of insults to the honour of the British nation and eventually convinced King George II to declare war on Spain. This war came to be known as 'The War of Jenkins' Ear'.

FRANÇOIS FÉNELON

(1651–1715, FRENCH THEOLOGIAN AND WRITER)

All wars are civil wars, because all men are brothers.

JOHN ARBUTHNOT 'JACKY' FISHER

(1841–1920, BRITISH ADMIRAL)

The essence of war is violence.
Moderation in war is imbecility.

All political parties die at last of
swallowing their own lies.

I have had to fight like hell and fighting
like hell has made me what I am.

TEXT ME, JACKY

JOHN ARBUTHNOT 'JACKY' FISHER was one of the
most celebrated officers in the history of the Royal
Navy. He was actively involved in the service of the
navy for over sixty years, starting his career during
the Crimean War and ending it during World War
One. From a comparatively poor background, he
made friends in the right places and forged his
way up through the ranks. He became a gunnery
expert, founded the navy's torpedo branch and
embarked upon a twenty-year period of reform.
His innovations – including the conception of the
battleship Dreadnought – had a huge influence in
modernising the navy and ensured its dominance
in World War One. Fisher also found time to
rewrite the training manuals and improve methods
of communication – he is even credited with being
the first to use OMG (in a letter to Churchill) as an
abbreviation for 'Oh, My God!' LOL.

M. F. K. FISHER

(1908–1992, AMERICAN WRITER)

War is a beastly business, it is true, but one
proof we are human is our ability to learn,
even from it, how better to exist.

JANET FLANNER

(1892–1978, AMERICAN JOURNALIST)

When you look at the startling ruins of Nuremberg, you are looking at a result of the war. When you look at the prisoners on view in the courthouse, you are looking at twenty-two of the causes.

*Speaking of the International Military
Tribunal in Nuremberg in 1946*

ABRAHAM FLEXNER

(1866–1959, AMERICAN EDUCATOR)

Probably, no nation is rich enough to pay for both war and civilisation. We must make our choice; we cannot have both.

FERDINAND FOCH

(1851–1929, FRENCH MARSHAL)

Hard pressed on my right. My centre is yielding. Impossible to manoeuvre. Situation excellent. I am attacking.

Battlefield report from the Battle of the Marne, 1914

The most powerful weapon on earth is the human soul on fire.

The will to conquer is the first condition of victory.

A battle won is a battle which we will
not acknowledge to be lost.

None but a coward dares to boast
that he has never known fear.

It takes 15,000 casualties to train a major general.

Aeroplanes are interesting toys
but of no military value.

HENRY FORD

(1863–1947, AMERICAN INDUSTRIALIST)

Wars do not end wars any more than
an extraordinarily large conflagration
does away with the fire hazard.

HONOR FORD-SMITH

(BORN 1951, JAMAICAN ACTRESS AND WRITER)

I fell and fell,
was lost, bled, marooned in a landscape
that grew stranger with each discovery I made.

*From 'A Message from Ni', describing how Nanny
of the Maroons, the Jamaican slave rebellion leader,
must have felt at the start of her campaign*

TWO BACARDI BREEZERS?
THAT'LL BE ONE NANNY

QUEEN NANNY OF THE Maroons, or 'Granny Nanny', was an Ashanti woman who had arrived in Jamaica as a slave from the Gold Coast (now Ghana) in West Africa. The British, who had captured Jamaica from the Spanish in 1655, ruled with an iron fist. Those slaves who escaped into the mountains were known as Maroons (from the Spanish word 'cimarron', meaning 'mountaintop dweller') and one of their greatest leaders was Nanny, who overcame her own feelings of displacement and injustice to fight throughout the First Maroon War until her death in 1733.

She became expert in guerrilla warfare, setting up camp high in the mountains so that the Maroons only had a single path to defend. She also became skilled in the art of camouflage and British soldiers often had their throats slit by the very trees or bushes they had stopped to rest against. Nanny was credited with freeing 800 slaves over a fifty-year period, and with causing the deaths of large numbers of British soldiers notwithstanding the very limited resources of the Maroons. Today she is immortalised in poetry and song and the Jamaican government declared her the country's only National Heroine in 1976. Her image adorns the Jamaican $500 bill, which is known as a 'Nanny', and will just about get you a couple of drinks at a bar in Kingston.

C. S. FORESTER

(1899–1966, ENGLISH WRITER)

Any ship can be a minesweeper once.

*Spoken by Horatio Hornblower, a fictional Royal
Navy officer in Forester's series of novels*

HARRY EMERSON FOSDICK

(1878–1969, AMERICAN CLERGYMAN)

The tragedy of war is that it uses
man's best to do man's worst.

ANATOLE FRANCE

(1844–1924, FRENCH POET AND JOURNALIST)

You think you are dying for your country;
you die for the industrialists.

FRANCISCO FRANCO

(1892–1975, SPANISH DICTATOR AND GENERAL)

The defence of internal peace and order constitutes
the sacred mission of a nation's armed forces
and that is what we have carried out.

One thing that I am sure of, and which I can answer
truthfully, is that whatever the contingencies that may
arise here, wherever I am there will be no Communism.

ANNE FRANK

(1929–1945, GERMAN DIARIST AND HOLOCAUST VICTIM)

I don't think of all the misery but of
the beauty that still remains.

I must uphold my ideals, for perhaps the time will
come when I shall be able to carry them out.

*Two entries from the diary that she kept while in hiding in
Nazi-occupied Holland from June 1942 to August 1944*

BENJAMIN FRANKLIN

(1706–1790, AMERICAN STATESMAN, SCIENTIST AND INVENTOR)

I have been apt to think that there has
never been, nor ever will be, any such
thing as a good war, or a bad peace.

Even peace may be purchased at too high a price.

They that can give up essential liberty to obtain a little
temporary safety, deserve neither liberty nor safety.

FREDERICK WILLIAM I

(1688–1740, KING OF PRUSSIA)

The most beautiful girl or woman in the world
would be a matter of indifference to me, but
tall soldiers – they are my weakness.

UNNECESSARILY TALL SOLDIERS

FREDERICK WILLIAM I OF **Prussia** was a man of obsessions, one of which led him to form the so-called Potsdam Giants, an infantry regiment of way-taller-than-average soldiers. He recruited them by any means possible: he bought them from the armies of other European countries; he paid fathers for their tallest sons; he paid bonuses to landowners to give up their tallest farm workers; he kidnapped Europe's tallest monks, priests and innkeepers. He even forced tall women to marry tall soldiers so that they could produce tall sons.

He never risked his giants in battle (they would, after all, have made for fairly easy targets), but he would train and drill them every day, show them off to foreign dignitaries at every opportunity, and even paint their portraits from memory on the few occasions they were let out of his sight. And we thought George III was mad.

FREDERICK II

(THE GREAT) (1712–1786, KING OF PRUSSIA)

Artillery adds dignity to what would otherwise be an ugly brawl.

Do not forget the dogs of war, your big guns, which are the most-to-be-respected arguments of the rights of kings.

When an officer comes on parade, every man in the barrack square should tremble in his shoes.

Without supplies, no army is brave.

Everything which the enemy least
expects will succeed the best.

The most certain way of insuring victory is to
march briskly and in good order against the
enemy, always endeavouring to gain ground.

SIGMUND FREUD

(1856–1939, AUSTRIAN NEUROLOGIST AND PSYCHOANALYST)

The tendency to aggression is an innate, independent,
instinctual disposition in man... it constitutes
the most powerful obstacle to culture.

A belligerent state permits itself every
such misdeed, every such act of violence,
as would disgrace the individual.

DAVID FRIEDMAN

(BORN 1945, AMERICAN ECONOMIST AND WRITER)

The direct use of force is such a poor solution
to any problem; it is generally employed only
by small children and large nations.

SEXTUS JULIUS FRONTINUS

(C. AD 40–103, ROMAN CHIEF MILITARY ENGINEER)

I will ignore all ideas for new works and engines of
war, the invention of which has reached its limits
and for whose improvement I see no further hope.

G

ADOLF GALLAND

(1912–1996, GERMAN LUFTWAFFE GENERAL AND FLYING ACE)

Never abandon the possibility of attack.
Attack even from a position of inferiority,
to disrupt the enemy's plans.

'He who wants to protect everything, protects
nothing' is one of the fundamental rules of defence.

The first rule of all air combat is to see the opponent
first. Like the hunter who stalks his prey.

Only the spirit of attack borne in a brave heart
will bring success to any fighter aircraft, no
matter how highly developed it may be.

Success… in the long run comes only to the one
who combines daring with cool thinking.

INDIRA GANDHI

(1917–1984, INDIAN PRIME MINISTER)

You can't shake hands with a clenched fist.

MOHANDAS KARAMCHAND GANDHI

(1869–1944, INDIAN CIVIL RIGHTS LEADER)

I am prepared to die, but there is no cause
for which I am prepared to kill.

What difference does it make to the dead, the orphans
and the homeless, whether the mad destruction
is wrought under the name of totalitarianism
or the holy name of liberty or democracy?

Victory attained by violence is tantamount
to a defeat, for it is momentary.

An eye for an eye only makes the whole world blind.

GIUSEPPE GARIBALDI

(1807–1882, ITALIAN REVOLUTIONARY LEADER)

Qui si fa l'Italia o si muore.
(Here we make Italy, or we die.)

Yes, young men, Italy owes to you an undertaking that
has merited the applause of the universe. You have
conquered and you will conquer still, because you are
prepared for the tactics that decide the fate of battles.

You, too, women, cast away all the cowards from your embraces; they will give you only cowards for children, and you who are the daughters of the land of beauty must bear children who are noble and brave.

I offer neither pay, nor quarters, nor food; I offer only hunger, thirst, forced marches, battles and death. Let him who loves his country with his heart, and not merely with his lips, follow me.

Three excerpts from speeches to encourage his troops and supporters during the campaign to unify Italy

THOMAS GASPEY

(1788–1871, ENGLISH WRITER AND JOURNALIST)

And now in England, just as gay –
As in the battle brave –
[He] goes to the rout, review, or play,
With one foot in the grave.

Writing about the Earl of Uxbridge's leg, which had been amputated following the Battle of Waterloo

CHARLES DE GAULLE

(1890–1970, FRENCH GENERAL AND STATESMAN)

Whatever happens, the flame of the French resistance must not be extinguished and will not be extinguished. Tomorrow, as today, I will speak on the radio from London.

Excerpt from de Gaulle's first broadcast from London on 18 June 1940

A LEG-END IN HIS OWN LIFETIME

THE STORY OF THE Earl of Uxbridge's Leg, as reported by Thomas Gaspey, is a great footnote to the Battle of Waterloo. Reputedly, when his leg was shot through with cannon, the Earl cried out: 'By God, sir, I've lost my leg!' to which the nearby Duke of Wellington replied: 'By God, sir, so you have!'

The unfortunate Earl was then rushed to British headquarters for the brutal amputation of his leg with a saw, long before the days of surgical anaesthesia. The amputated leg was buried in the village of Waterloo, and its 'tomb' became a rather offbeat tourist attraction for those who learned of Uxbridge's brave fatalism. The inscription on the 'tombstone' began:

'Here lies the Leg of the illustrious
and valiant Earl Uxbridge, Lieutenant-
General of His Britannic Majesty.'

The leg attracted a bewildering range of tourists from the top drawer of European society, including the King of Prussia and the Prince of Orange. The rest of the Earl went on to serve his country in a variety of posts for almost another 40 years, which is an admirably long time to have one foot in the grave.

A true leader always keeps an element of surprise up his sleeve, which others cannot grasp but which keeps his public excited and breathless.

France cannot be France without greatness.

To deliberate is the act of many.
To act is the act of one.

Faced with crisis, the man of character falls back
on himself. He imposes his own stamp of action,
takes responsibility for it, makes it his own.

It's true that, sometimes, the military does abuse its
power relative to intelligence, by neglecting to use any.

Only peril can bring the French together. One
can't impose unity out of the blue on a country
that has 265 different kinds of cheese.

War is like hunting with the exception
that in war the rabbits shoot back.

JAMES M. GAVIN

(1907–1990, AMERICAN ARMY GENERAL)

Show me a man who'll jump out of an aeroplane,
and I'll show you a man who'll fight.

Never in the history of war have so
few been led by so many.

*Referring to an occasion in Sicily when, after some units
became separated, Gavin joined ranks with two colonels, a
major, three captains, two lieutenants and one rifleman.*

W. L. GEORGE

(1882–1926, ANGLO-FRENCH WRITER)

Wars teach us not to love our enemies,
but to hate our allies.

DAVID LLOYD GEORGE

(1863–1945, BRITISH PRIME MINISTER)

At eleven o'clock this morning came to an end
the cruellest and most terrible war that has ever
scourged mankind. I hope we may say that thus,
this fateful morning, came to an end all wars.

Speech in the House of Commons, 11 November 1918

What is our task? To make Britain a
fit country for heroes to live in.

November 1918

Believe me, Germany is unable to wage war.

August 1934

When the Great War broke out our Generals had
the most important lessons of their art to learn.

War Memoirs

Once blood is shed in a national quarrel reason and
right are swept aside by the rage of angry men.

Don't be afraid to take a big step if one is indicated.
You can't cross a chasm in two small jumps.

You are not going to get peace with millions
of armed men. The chariot of peace cannot
advance over a road littered with cannon.

GEORGE III

(1738–1820, KING OF GREAT BRITAIN AND IRELAND)

Mad, is he? Then I hope he will bite
some of my other generals!

Referring to General Wolfe (and the indecision of his other generals)

Once vigorous measures appear to be the only means
left of bringing the Americans to a due submission
to the mother country, the colonies will submit.

GEORGE V

(1865–1936, KING OF THE UNITED KINGDOM AND THE
BRITISH DOMINIONS, AND EMPEROR OF INDIA)

I have many times asked myself whether there can
be more potent advocates of peace upon earth
through the years to come than this massed multitude
of silent witnesses to the desolation of war.

Speaking at a World War One cemetery in Flanders in 1922

I may be uninspiring, but I'll be damned if I'm alien.

*In response to H. G. Wells' reference during
World War One to Britain's 'alien and uninspiring
court' ('alien' in the sense of Germanic)*

WHAT'S IN A NAME, BY GEORGE?

GEORGE V, PRIOR TO his coronation in 1910, had led a relatively carefree existence serving in the navy and preparing to be king. He was best known for his obsessive stamp collecting and industrial-scale shooting of pheasants and tigers. The British public warmed to him when he took to touring the front lines during World War One, thereby displaying a firm stance against his cousin and look-alike Kaiser Wilhelm II. He became even more popular towards the end of the war, when he changed the family name from Saxe-Coburg-Gotha to Windsor in order to distance the Royal Family from its German ancestry (and probably also to stop H. G. Wells sniping about his origins). This name change was to prove especially useful to the monarchy between 1939 and 1945.

GEORGE VI

(1895–1952, KING OF THE UNITED KINGDOM AND THE DOMINIONS OF THE BRITISH COMMONWEALTH)

It is not the walls that make the city, but the people who live within them. The walls of London may be battered, but the spirit of the Londoner stands resolute and undismayed.

During the Blitz in World War Two

Germany, the enemy who drove all Europe into
war, has been finally overcome. In the Far East we
have yet to deal with the Japanese, a determined
and cruel foe. To this we shall turn with the
utmost resolve and with all our resources.

Let us remember the men in all the services, and the
women in all the services, who have laid down their
lives. We have come to the end of our tribulation and
they are not with us at the moment of our rejoicing.

Our cause was the cause not of this nation only,
not of this Empire and Commonwealth only,
but of every land where freedom is cherished
and law and liberty go hand in hand.

Three excerpts from his address to the nation on 8 May 1945

DAVID GERROLD

(BORN 1944, AMERICAN WRITER)

The only winner in the war of 1812 was Tchaikovsky.

The War Against the Chtorr

EDWARD GIBBON

(1737–1794, ENGLISH HISTORIAN AND POLITICIAN)

As long as mankind shall continue to bestow
more liberal applause on their destroyers than on
their benefactors, the thirst of military glory will
ever be the vice of the most exalted characters.

JEAN GIRAUDOUX

(1882–1944, FRENCH PLAYWRIGHT)

As soon as war is declared it will be impossible to hold the poets back. Rhyme is still the most effective drum.

JOSEPH GOEBBELS

(1897–1945, GERMAN MINISTER OF PROPAGANDA)

The essence of propaganda consists in winning people over to an idea so sincerely, so vitally, that in the end they succumb to it utterly and can never again escape from it.

If you repeat a lie often enough, it becomes the truth.

Talking about British propaganda tactics

We can do without butter, but, despite all our love of peace, not without arms. One cannot shoot with butter, but with guns.

The war is not only a great equaliser, it is a great educator. Only what is essential can survive its hard laws. It transforms all values. Things that we thought important or even essential during peace, we gladly give up during war to serve the common cause.

Future historians will wonder how it was possible for their peoples to believe in a good outcome and a coming victory, despite eternal defeats along the way.

Writing in June 1942 about the Allies' non-existent chances of success

We are not like the English plutocrats who teach their young children to wear frock coats and top hats. Anyone who needs to do that later can learn how later. We are teaching our youth what is difficult to learn later, namely attitude and character.

HERMANN GOERING

(1893–1946, GERMAN MILITARY LEADER)

My Luftwaffe is invincible… And so now we turn to England. How long will this one last – two, three weeks?
Speaking in June 1940 about the imminent Battle of Britain

Voice or no voice, the people can always be brought to the bidding of the leaders. That is easy. All you have to do is to tell them they are being attacked, and denounce the pacifists for lack of patriotism and exposing the country to danger. It works the same in any country.

I considered the attacks on London useless, and I told the Führer again and again that inasmuch as I knew the English people as well as I did my own people, I could never force them to their knees by attacking London. We might be able to subdue the Dutch people by such measures but not the British.
Speaking at the International Military Tribunal in Nuremberg, 1946

No enemy bomber can reach the Ruhr. If one reaches the Ruhr, my name is not Goering. You may call me Meyer.
Addressing the Luftwaffe in September 1939

Above all, I shall see to it that the enemy
will not be able to drop any bombs.

JOHANN WOLFGANG VON GOETHE

(1749–1832, GERMAN WRITER)

Divide and rule, a sound motto.
Unite and lead, a better one.

ARTHUR GOLDEN

(BORN 1956, AMERICAN WRITER)

A mind troubled by doubt cannot
focus on the course to victory.

BARRY GOLDWATER

(1909–1998, AMERICAN SENATOR)

You don't have to be straight to be in the military;
you just have to be able to shoot straight.

ULYSSES S. GRANT

(1822–1885, EIGHTEENTH PRESIDENT OF THE UNITED STATES)

The art of war is simple enough. Find out where
your enemy is. Get at him as soon as you can. Strike
him as hard as you can, and keep moving on.

I have never advocated war except as a means of peace.

In every battle there comes a time when
both sides consider themselves beaten, then
he who continues the attack wins.

If you see the President, tell him from me that
whatever happens there will be no turning back.

I propose to fight it out on this
line if it takes all summer.

I have made it a rule of my life to trust a man long
after other people gave him up, but I don't see
how I can ever trust any human being again.

THOMAS GRAY

(1716–1771, ENGLISH POET AND PROFESSOR)

The paths of glory lead but to the grave.

*From 'Elegy in a Country Churchyard' and recited by General James
Wolfe the evening before he died in battle on the Plains of Abraham*

The time will come, when thou shalt lift thine eyes
To watch a long-drawn battle in the skies.
While aged peasants, too amazed for words,
Stare at the flying fleets of wondrous birds.
England, so long mistress of the sea,
Where winds and waves confess her sovereignty,
Her ancient triumphs yet on high shall bear
And reign the sovereign of the conquered air.

*Prophetic words that seem to foretell the Battle of
Britain, from 'Luna Habitabilis' in 1737*

EDWARD GREY

(1862–1933, BRITISH FOREIGN SECRETARY)

The lamps are going out all over Europe. We shall not see them lit again in our time.

The British Army should be a projectile to be fired by the British Navy.

ERNESTO 'CHE' GUEVARA

(1928–1967, ARGENTINIAN
REVOLUTIONARY AND GUERRILLA LEADER)

I don't care if I fall as long as someone else picks up my gun and keeps on shooting.

The revolution is not an apple that falls when it is ripe. You have to make it fall.

Cruel leaders are replaced only to have new leaders turn cruel.

Hasta la victoria siempre!
(Until the everlasting victory!)

I know you are here to kill me. Shoot, coward, you are only going to kill a man.
Reportedly his last words

Other regions of the world claim the support of
my modest efforts. I can do what is forbidden
to you because of your responsibility to Cuba,
and the time has come for us to separate.

From 'Che' Guevara's farewell letter to Fidel Castro in 1965

A REBEL WITH TOO MANY CAUSES?

BY THE TIME THE Argentinian Guevara arrived in
Cuba with the Castro brothers in 1956, he had
already fought for the Marxist cause in Guatemala
and trained in guerrilla warfare with Cuban exiles
in Mexico. Over the next three years he was
instrumental in overthrowing the United-States-
backed Batista regime in Cuba and he served in a
number of government posts for Fidel Castro for
six years after that. He then decided that it was
time to sort out the rest of the world. He started
(without much success) in the Democratic Republic
of the Congo, offered to help some other rebels
in Mozambique (they turned the offer down) and
then moved on to Bolivia, where he did meet with
some success before the CIA-backed government
there brought about his capture and execution.

His life is immortalised today not just in history
books, but also on countless T-shirts, posters,
mugs, ornaments, dolls, puppets, calendars, berets,
beer mats and baseball boots. Go capitalism!

H

HERMANN HAGEDORN

(1882–1964, AMERICAN WRITER)

The bomb that fell on Hiroshima fell on
America too. It fell on no city, no munition
plants, no docks. It erased no church, vaporised
no public buildings, reduced no man to
his atomic elements. But it fell, it fell.

DOUGLAS HAIG

(1861–1928, BRITISH ARMY GENERAL)

Almost all aspects of the art of war are
'theoretical' in time of peace; they only become
'practical' when the actual killing begins.

From a letter to Churchill, January 1914

Further, a defensive policy involves the loss
of the initiative, with all the consequent
disadvantages to the defender.

There can be no question that to our general
unpreparedness must be attributed the loss
of many thousands of brave men whose
sacrifice we deeply deplore, while we regard
their gallantry with unstinted admiration.

NATHAN HALE

(1755–1776, AMERICAN SOLDIER AND SPY)

I only regret that I have but one
life to give for my country.

Last words just before his execution by the British

EVELYN BEATRICE HALL

(1868–C. 1939, ENGLISH WRITER)

I disapprove of what you say, but I will
defend to the death your right to say it.

*In her biography of Voltaire,
The Friends of Voltaire*

WILLIAM HALSEY JR

(1882–1959, AMERICAN NAVAL OFFICER)

Cease firing, but if any enemy planes appear,
shoot them down in friendly fashion.

*Message to Third Fleet at sea off Tokyo, after
Japanese surrender on 15 August 1945*

ALEXANDER HAMILTON

(1755–1804, SECRETARY OF THE TREASURY OF THE UNITED STATES)

When the sword is drawn, the passions of
men observe no bounds of moderation.

JACK HANDEY

(BORN 1949, AMERICAN HUMORIST)

Instead of building newer and larger weapons
of mass destruction, I think mankind should
try to get more use out of the ones we have.

HANNIBAL

(247–182 BC, COMMANDER-IN-CHIEF OF THE CARTHAGINIAN ARMY)

God has given to man no sharper spur
to victory than contempt of death.

I will either find a way, or make one.
On the need to get his army over the Alps

THOMAS HARDY

(1840–1928, ENGLISH WRITER)

War makes rattling good history;
but Peace is poor reading.

I'LL SET HANNIBAL ON YOU
IF YOU DON'T BEHAVE!

HANNIBAL IS OF COURSE best known for crossing the Alps during the Second Punic War with thousands of foot soldiers and horsemen, and quite a few elephants. Make no mistake, though, Hannibal was not a one-hit wonder. For almost twenty years, he proved himself a supreme military commander and tactician, winning battle after battle against powerful armies and experienced generals, including those of the mighty Roman Empire. Such was the fear that he struck into the Roman psyche that parents would threaten their children with him whenever they misbehaved. His achievements were all the more astonishing when you consider that he never really received that much support from his home city of Carthage, thereby forcing him to replenish his army time and again in foreign lands, including Iberia and Gaul. That's a bit like a foreign football manager winning the Champions League with an English team full of players from a number of different countries – it just couldn't happen!

ARTHUR 'BOMBER' HARRIS

(1892–1984, MARSHAL OF THE ROYAL AIR FORCE)

We are going to scourge the Third Reich from end to end. We are bombing Germany city by city and ever more terribly in order to make it impossible for her to go on with the war. That is our object, and we shall pursue it relentlessly.

The Nazis entered this war under the rather childish illusion that they were going to bomb everyone else, and that nobody was going to bomb them… They sowed the wind and now they are going to reap the whirlwind.

Two extracts from speeches from Bomber Command in World War Two

VÁCLAV HAVEL

(1936–2011, CZECH PRESIDENT)

To respond to evil by committing another evil does not eliminate evil but allows it to go on forever.

CHARLES HAY

(1700–1760, BRITISH GENERAL)

Gentlemen of France, perhaps you would care to fire first?

At the start of the Battle of Fontenoy, 1745, during the War of the Austrian Succession

JOSEPH HELLER

(1923–1999, AMERICAN WRITER)

Frankly, I'd like to see the government
get out of war altogether and leave the
whole field to private individuals.

Catch 22

CLAUDE HELVÉTIUS

(1715–1771, FRENCH PHILOSOPHER)

Discipline is simply the art of making the soldiers
fear their officers more than the enemy.

ERNEST HEMINGWAY

(1899–1961, AMERICAN WRITER AND WAR CORRESPONDENT)

Never think that war, no matter how necessary,
nor how justified, is not a crime.

Wars are caused by undefended wealth.

There is nothing sweet nor fitting in your dying. You
will die like a dog for no good reason.

The sinews of war are five – men, money,
materials, maintenance (food) and morale.

No catalogue of horrors ever kept men from war.

FROM HEMINGWAY TO COLVIN

ERNEST HEMINGWAY SPENT TWO months at the age of eighteen as a volunteer ambulance driver at the Italian Front in World War One. Two months in that job were enough for him to witness first hand the dreadfulness of war – and to get seriously wounded by mortar fire. Despite his wounds, he carried an Italian soldier to safety, for which he received the Italian Silver Medal for Bravery. None of that put him off a future career as a war reporter, in which role he most notably covered the Spanish Civil War (on which experience he based his novel *For Whom the Bells Toll*) and World War Two, including the Normandy landings. In 1947 he was awarded the Bronze Star for 'bravery under fire in order to obtain an accurate and vivid account of the difficulties and horrors of battle'. There remain many such reporters in the world's trouble spots today, of course, and the death of Marie Colvin, a journalist for *The Sunday Times*, in Syria in February 2012 reminded the world of the dangers they face.

ARCHIBALD HENDERSON

(1783–1859, UNITED STATES MARINE CORPS COMMANDER)

Have gone to Florida to fight Indians. Back when war is over.

Notice pinned on his office door in 1836 before leaving to fight against the rebellious Creek and Seminole Indian tribes in Georgia and Florida

HERMOCRATES

(DIED 407 BC, SYRACUSAN GENERAL)

Where there is mutual fear, men think twice
before they make aggression upon one another.

They have an abundance of gold and silver, and
these make war, like other things, go smoothly.

Nobody is driven in to war by ignorance,
and no one who thinks he will gain
anything from it is deterred by fear.

HERODOTUS

(C. 484–425 BC, GREEK HISTORIAN)

In peace, sons bury their fathers. In
war, fathers bury their sons.

Far better it is to have a stout heart always
and suffer one's share of evils, than to
be ever fearing what may happen.

GEORGE STILLMAN HILLARD

(1808–1879, AMERICAN LAWYER AND WRITER)

No man can be a great officer who is
not infinitely patient of details, for an
army is an aggregation of details.

Life and Campaigns of George B. McLellan

HIPPOCRATES

(C. 460–370 BC, GREEK PHYSICIAN)

War is the only proper school of the surgeon.

HIROHITO

(1901–1989, EMPEROR OF JAPAN)

All men are brothers, like the seas throughout
the world; so why do winds and waves
clash so fiercely everywhere?

We have resolved to endure the unendurable
and suffer what is insufferable.

ADOLF HITLER

(1889–1945, GERMAN FÜHRER)

Strength lies not in defence but in attack.

Demoralise the enemy from within by surprise, terror,
sabotage, assassination. This is the war of the future.

Chamberlain seemed such a nice old gentleman
that I thought I would give him my autograph.

Where Napoleon failed, I shall succeed; I
shall land on the shores of Britain.

The broad masses of a nation... more readily
fall victim to the big lie than the small lie.

Mein Kampf

Whoever lights the torch of war in Europe
can wish for nothing but chaos.

The victor will never be asked if he told the truth.

For there is one thing we must never forget... the
majority can never replace the man. And no more
than a hundred empty heads make one wise man will
an heroic decision arise from a hundred cowards.

The woman has her own battlefield. With
every child she brings into the world
she fights a battle for the nation.

WOULD YOU TRUST A
TEETOTAL VEGETARIAN?

IT IS WELL KNOWN that Hitler greatly admired the
handsome and fit youth of Germany, but not
everyone knows what a fine example of healthy
living he was himself. He didn't drink much, if at
all, he was strongly opposed to smoking and he was,
by most accounts, firmly vegetarian. He did enjoy a
cream cake or a bar of chocolate from time to time,
but that was pretty much his only vice, at least as
far as personal health was concerned. It has been
claimed that he was vegetarian because he couldn't
stomach the thought of poor animals suffering and
it is certainly the case that he loved his Alsatians.
Apparently he also enjoyed a spot of birdwatching.
In fact, he was almost too good to be true, you
might think in your more cynical moments.

J. D. Hittle

(1915–2002, United States Marines brigadier general)

If the history of military organisation proves anything, it is that those units that are told they are second class will almost inevitably prove that they are second class.

Ho Chi Minh

(1890–1969, Vietnamese leader)

You can kill ten of our men for every one we kill of yours. But even at those odds, you will lose and we will win.

Addressed to the French when war was looming in 1946

In the face of United States aggression [the Vietnamese people] have risen up, united as one man.

Homer

(c. eighth century bc, Greek epic poet)

Even the bravest cannot fight beyond his strength.

Noble and manly music invigorates the spirit, strengthens the wavering man, and incites him to great and worthy deeds.

To those that flee comes neither power nor glory.

Men grow tired of sleep, love, singing and dancing sooner than war.

A glorious death is his who for his country falls.

Zeus most glorious and most great, Thundercloud,
throned in the heavens! Let not the sun go down
and the darkness come, until I cast down headlong
the citadel of Priam in flames, and burn his gates
with blazing fire, and tear to rags the shirt upon
Hector's breast! May many of his men fall about him
prone in the dry dust and bite the brown earth!

The Iliad

WILLIAM HOOKE

(1612–1652, BRITISH COLONIAL GOVERNOR)

A day of battle is a day of harvest for the devil.

HERBERT HOOVER

(1874–1964, THIRTY-FIRST PRESIDENT OF THE UNITED STATES)

Older men declare war. But it is the
youth that must fight and die.

It is a paradox that every dictator has climbed
to power on the ladder of free speech.
Immediately on attaining power each dictator
has suppressed all free speech except his own.

It is the youth who must inherit the tribulation, the
sorrow and the triumphs that are the aftermath of war.

Peace is not made at the council table or
by treaties, but in the hearts of men.

HORACE

(65–8 BC, ROMAN POET)

Bella detesta matribus. (Wars, the horror of mothers.)

Dulce et decorum est pro patria mori. (It is a sweet and seemly thing to die for one's country.)

SAM HOUSTON

(1793–1863, AMERICAN ARMY GENERAL AND STATESMAN)

Remember the Alamo!

Battle cry of the Texans at San Jacinto in 1836 when they took their revenge for the Alamo by wiping out hundreds of unprepared Mexicans in approximately eighteen minutes

VICTOR HUGO

(1802–1885, FRENCH WRITER)

A day will come when a cannon will be exhibited in museums, just as instruments of torture are now, and the people will be astonished that such a thing could have been.

Civil war? What does that mean? Is there any foreign war? Isn't every war fought between men, between brothers?

There have been in this century only one great man and one great thing: Napoleon and liberty. For want of the great man, let us have the great thing.

An invasion of armies can be resisted, but
not an idea whose time has come.

A war between Europeans is a civil war.

Peace is the virtue of civilisation. War is its crime.

REX HUNT

(BORN 1926, BRITISH DIPLOMAT AND GOVERNOR
OF THE FALKLAND ISLANDS)

This is British territory. You're not invited.
We don't want you here. I want you to go
now and take all your men with you.

*Addressed to Admiral Carlos Busser, commander
of the Argentine invasion force in 1982*

CHRISTIAAN HUYGENS

(1629–1695, DUTCH ASTRONOMER)

How vast those Orbs must be, and how inconsiderable
this Earth, the Theatre upon which all our mighty
Designs, all our Navigations, and all our Wars are
transacted, when compared to them. A very fit
Consideration, and matter of Reflection, for those
Kings and Princes who sacrifice the Lives of so
many People, only to flatter their Ambition in being
Masters of some pitiful corner of this small Spot.

The Celestial Worlds Discover'd

I

DOLORES IBÁRRURI

(LA PASIONARIA) (1895–1989, SPANISH REPUBLICAN
LEADER AND COMMUNIST POLITICIAN)

Workers! Farmers! Antifascists! Patriotic Spaniards!
Everyone rise to defend the Republic against the
Fascist military uprising, to defend the common
freedoms and the democratic triumphs of the people!

Stand up, people of Spain! Women! Defend
the lives of your children, defend the liberty of
your men! Endure every conceivable sacrifice
rather than grant the victory of the forces which
represent a past of oppression, a past of tyranny.

No pasarán! (They shall not pass.)

*At the Battle of Madrid in November 1936. The siege of Madrid
would last for two and a half years, when the Communist
forces were finally defeated by General Franco's Nationalists.*

It is better to be the widow of a hero
than the wife of a coward.

Dawn is breaking over Spain, and that dawn,
scattering the darkness of the past, is the dawning
of a Spain where the people will be the leading
actor, where once more the rights of men and
of the peoples who make up our multi-national
and multi-regional country will be respected.

Upon General Franco's death in 1975

HENRIK IBSEN

(1828–1906, NORWEGIAN PLAYWRIGHT)

You should never wear your best trousers when
you go out to fight for freedom and truth.

MICHAEL IGNATIEFF

(BORN 1947, CANADIAN WRITER)

The wars of the future will be fought
by computer technicians and by lawyers
and high-altitude specialists.

There's a financial cost, but the only costs that
are ever real are the costs of our soldiers.

WILLIAM INGE

(1860–1954, ENGLISH WRITER AND PRIEST)

The enemies of freedom do not argue;
they shout and they shoot.

A man may build himself a throne of
bayonets, but he cannot sit on it.

JEAN INGELOW

(1820–1897, ENGLISH WRITER)

And O the buttercups! that field
O' the cloth of gold, when pennons swam –
Where France set up his lilied shield,
His oriflamb,
And Henry's lion-standard rolled:
What was it to their matchless sheen,
Their million million drops of gold
Among the green!

From 'The Letter L. – Present'

KAI KA'US IBN ISKANDAR

(ELEVENTH CENTURY, PERSIAN PRINCE)

Once you engage in battle it is inexcusable to
display any sloth or hesitation; you must breakfast
on your enemy before he dines on you.

IVAN THE TERRIBLE

(1530–1584, RUSSIAN RULER)

I will not see the destruction of the
Christian converts who are loyal to me, and to my
last breath I will fight for the Orthodox faith.

MY CODPIECE IS BIGGER THAN YOURS

THE POEM, 'THE LETTER L. – Present' by Jean Ingelow refers to a meeting between France and England at 'the Field of the Cloth of Gold'. In 1518 the Treaty of London was signed as a pact of non-aggression by some of the major European leaders of the time, including Henry VIII of England, Francis I of France and Charles V, the Holy Roman Emperor. The pact was soon in danger of falling apart so Cardinal Wolsey set up bilateral meetings for Henry to establish closer political bonds, first with the Holy Roman Emperor and then, in June 1520, near Calais, with Francis I. So lavish were the camps set up to house the vast retinues on both sides that history records the meeting place as the Field of the Cloth of Gold (*le Camp du Drap d'Or*), and it is said that the costs involved came close to bankrupting both countries.

It soon became clear that the two and a half weeks would be spent establishing which of the two young kings had the larger codpiece, so to speak. Henry outshone Francis when it came to jousting, but Francis took Henry down in a wrestling match. Within a month, Henry had sided with the Holy Roman Emperor, and England was soon at war with France again. Plus ça change.

J

Thomas Jonathan 'Stonewall' Jackson

(1824–1863, American Civil War Confederate general)

My idea is that the best mode of fighting is to reserve your fire until the enemy get to close quarters. Then deliver one deadly, deliberate fire – and charge!

To move swiftly, strike vigorously, and secure all the fruits of victory, is the secret of successful war.

You appear much concerned about my attacking on Sunday. I am greatly concerned, too: but I felt it my duty to do it.

Letter to his wife from Virginia in 1862. Being deeply religious, he and his wife were greatly troubled by fighting on a Sunday.

It is painful enough to discover with what unconcern they speak of war and threaten it. I have seen enough of it to make me look upon it as the sum of all evils.

DOES MY ARM LOOK SHORT IN THIS?

'STONEWALL' JACKSON WAS ONE of the most remarkable characters of the American Civil War; a complex mixture of odd personality traits combined with frequent success in battle. He did not look like a brilliant leader in his unkempt uniform, often with one arm raised to the sky to restore the equilibrium he felt he lacked as a result of having one arm shorter than the other; a habit which on one occasion caused him to be shot in the middle finger. But he did prove to be a brilliant tactical commander and his 1862 Valley Campaign and his flanking of the Union army at Chancellorsville the following year are studied worldwide even today as examples of innovative and bold leadership.

He was accidentally shot by his own Confederate pickets after the battle at Chancellorsville, resulting in the immediate amputation of an arm and death by pneumonia eight days later. His death was considered a devastating blow to the morale and military prospects of the Confederacy. We'll never know whether the amputation would have been a good thing or a bad thing as far as his equilibrium was concerned.

My troops may fail to take a position,
but are never driven from one!

The patriot volunteer, fighting for country and his rights, makes the most reliable soldier on earth.

Arms is a profession that, if its principles are adhered to for success, requires an officer do what he fears may be wrong, and yet, according to military experience, must be done, if success is to be attained.

Under divine blessing, we must rely on the bayonet when firearms cannot be furnished.

War means fighting. The business of the soldier is to fight. Armies are not called out to dig trenches, to throw up breastworks, to live in camps, but to find the enemy and strike him; to invade his country, and do him all possible damage in the shortest possible time.

This coat is too handsome for me to wear, but I will cherish it as a souvenir.

Upon being presented with a fine general's uniform before the Battle of Fredericksburg

THOMAS JEFFERSON

(1743–1826, THIRD PRESIDENT OF THE UNITED STATES)

The power of making war often prevents it.

I have seen enough of one war never to wish to see another.

The tree of liberty must be refreshed from time to time with the blood of patriots and tyrants.

War is an instrument entirely inefficient toward redressing wrong: and multiplies, instead of indemnifying, losses.

As our enemies have found we can reason like men,
so now let us show them we can fight like men also.

Every citizen should be a soldier. This was
the case with the Greeks and Romans,
and must be that of every free state.

The most successful war seldom pays for its losses.

The world is indebted for all triumphs
that have been gained by reason and
humanity over error and oppression.

I recoil with horror at the ferociousness of
man. Will nations never devise a more rational
umpire of differences than force? Are there no
means of coercing injustice more gratifying to our
nature than a waste of the blood of thousands?

RICHARD JENI

(1957–2007, AMERICAN COMEDIAN AND ACTOR)

You're basically killing each other to see
who's got the better imaginary friend.

On going to war over religion

JIANG QING

(1914–1991, CHINESE REVOLUTIONARY
LEADER AND WIFE OF MAO ZEDONG)

I was Chairman Mao's dog. What he said to bite, I bit.

There cannot be peaceful coexistence in the
ideological realm. Peaceful coexistence corrupts.

JOAN OF ARC

(JEANNE D'ARC) (C. 1412–1431, FRENCH PEASANT
GIRL, MILITARY LEADER AND SAINT)

King of England, and you, Duke of Bedford, who call
yourself regent of the kingdom of France... settle your
debt to the king of Heaven; return to the Maiden,
who is envoy of the king of Heaven, the keys to all
the good towns you took and violated in France.

Of the love or hatred God has for the English, I
know nothing, but I do know that they will all be
thrown out of France, except those who die there.

I am not afraid; I was born to do this.

You, men of England, who have no right to this
Kingdom of France, the King of Heaven orders and
notifies you through me, Joan the Maiden, to leave
your fortresses and go back to your own country;
or I will produce a clash of arms to be eternally
remembered. And this is the third and last time I have
written to you; I shall not write anything further.

*Final warning to the English before Joan of Arc led
her troops against them at Orléans in 1429*

FROM RAGS TO VICTORY, MARTYRDOM AND SAINTHOOD

WHEN JOAN OF ARC was a peasant girl in her teens, the Hundred Years' War was well underway and the French hadn't won a decisive battle in living memory. Internal strife between Charles of Orléans and Philip the Good of Burgundy had encouraged Henry V to reinvade, at which point Philip sided with the English.

In the meantime, Joan was being visited by saints and angels, one of them telling her that Charles was in fact the rightful heir to the throne and that the English had to be driven out of France. By the time she was seventeen, she had convinced Charles that God was on his side and that she was to lead his troops into battle. The defeat of the English at Orléans was the first of a number of staggering successes that, at least for a while, turned the tide of the war. The Maid of Orléans, as she was now known, even secured the throne for Charles, but her subsequent capture soon brought things to a halt. She was tried and burned at the stake for heresy, at the age of nineteen.

When the English finally left France around 1450, the Catholic Church saw fit to reverse the heresy conviction, ultimately paving the way for Joan's sainthood in 1920. As apologies go, that was a big one.

ROBERT S. JOHNSON

(1920–1998, AMERICAN AIR FORCE FIGHTER
PILOT AND LIEUTENANT COLONEL)

Nothing makes a man more aware of his capabilities
and of his limitations than those moments when he
must push aside all the familiar defences of ego and
vanity, and accept reality by staring, with the fear that
is normal to a man in combat, into the face of Death.

The man who enters combat encased in solid
armor plate, but lacking the essential of self-
confidence, is far more exposed and naked to
death than the individual who subjects himself to
battle shorn of any protection but his own skill,
his own belief in himself and in his wingman.

SAMUEL JOHNSON

(1709–1784, ENGLISH WRITER)

To a people warlike and indigent, an incursion
into a rich country is never hurtful.

No man will be a sailor who has contrivance
enough to get himself into a jail; for being in
a ship is being in jail, with a chance of being
drowned… A man in a jail has more room,
better food, and commonly better company.

Treating your adversary with respect
is striking soft in battle.

Every man thinks meanly of himself
for not having been a soldier.

Letter to James Boswell, 1778

JOHN PAUL JONES

(1747–1792, SCOTTISH SAILOR AND AMERICAN NAVAL HERO)

I have not yet begun to fight!

*When asked if he was prepared to surrender at
the Battle of Flamborough Head in 1779, whilst
his boat was sinking and outgunned*

An honourable Peace is and always was my first
wish! I can take no delight in the effusion of
human Blood; but, if this War should continue,
I wish to have the most active part in it.

It seems to be a law of nature, inflexible and
inexorable, that those who will not risk cannot win.

I wish to have no connection with any ship that
does not sail fast; for I intend to go in harm's way.

THE SOMEWHAT CHEQUERED
CAREER OF JOHN PAUL JONES

JOHN PAUL JONES WAS born into poverty in Scotland in 1747 and ended up in an unmarked grave in Paris forty-five years later. What happened in between was remarkable. His apprenticeship at sea took him to Barbados and Virginia and was followed by a spell in the slave trade. By the time he joined the Continental Navy of the American Colonies in 1775 to fight the British, he had been acquitted of the murder of a ship's carpenter and had killed the ringleader of a mutiny in the West Indies. He was essentially a short man with a violent temper, and he would probably have played at right half for the Scottish football team if he hadn't gone to sea.

But he then proceeded to distinguish himself as a naval officer to the extent that he was awarded a gold medal by the Continental Congress, a gold sword by Louis XVI of France, and the position of Rear Admiral in the Russian Navy by Catherine the Great!

In 1905 his body was rediscovered after an extensive search and returned to America to be buried with full military honours at Annapolis Naval Academy. He is known to this day as the 'Father of the American Navy'.

K

Franz Kafka

(1883–1924, German writer)

Every revolution evaporates and leaves behind
only the slime of a new bureaucracy.

Paul Kagame

(born 1957, Rwandan president)

We cannot turn the clock back, nor can we
undo the harm caused, but we have the power
to determine the future and to ensure that
what happened never happens again.

Speaking of the genocide in Rwanda

A. P. J. Abdul Kalam

(born 1931, Indian president)

No religion has mandated killing others as a requirement for its sustenance or promotion.

Mikhail Kalashnikov

(born 1919, Russian small arms designer)

I made it to protect the motherland.

I'm proud of my invention, but I'm sad that it is used by terrorists.
Both referring to the AK-47

Philip Kearny

(1815–1862, American army officer)

I can make men follow me to hell.

The rebel bullet that can kill me has not yet been moulded.

War is horrible because it strangles youth.

George F. Kennan

(1904–2005, American diplomat and historian)

The American military-industrial establishment would have to go on, substantially unchanged, until some other adversary could be invented.
On the eventuality of the Soviet Union's sinking under the waters of the ocean

CLAUDIA KENNEDY

(BORN 1947, FIRST FEMALE THREE-STAR
GENERAL IN THE AMERICAN ARMY)

The Army damages itself when it
doesn't live up to its own values.

JOHN F. KENNEDY

(1917–1963, THIRTY-FIFTH PRESIDENT OF THE UNITED STATES)

Let every nation know, whether it wishes us well
or ill, that we shall pay any price, bear any burden,
meet any hardship, support any friend, oppose any
foe, to assure the survival and success of liberty.

In the long history of the world, only a few
generations have been granted the role of defending
freedom in its hour of maximum danger. I do not
shrink from this responsibility – I welcome it.

Let us never negotiate out of fear. But
let us never fear to negotiate.

My fellow Americans, ask not what your country can
do for you – ask what you can do for your country.
Four excerpts from his Inaugural Address, 20 January 1961

Victory has a thousand fathers, but defeat is an orphan.
*In accepting full personal responsibility for the
failed Bay of Pigs invasion in 1961*

CENTRAL WHAT AGENCY?

ALTHOUGH KENNEDY MAGNANIMOUSLY ACCEPTED full responsibility for the failed Bay of Pigs invasion, it is said that behind closed doors he was furious at what he saw as the incompetence of the CIA to pull off the operation. The world was to come to the brink of nuclear war the following year with the stand-off that would become known as the Cuban Missile Crisis and the ensuing decades would see America in general and the CIA in particular become obsessed with the uncomfortable proximity of Castro's Communist-backed regime. It may be as well that Kennedy did not live to see the whole gamut of CIA attempts to discredit or assassinate Castro in the years ahead, many of which have become the stuff of folklore. These allegedly included the poisoning of Castro's cigars, placing explosive seashells in his favourite diving spots, and sneaking thallium salts into his shoes in order to make his beard, eyebrows and pubic hair fall out! A United States Senate Committee in 1975 confirmed at least eight attempts on Castro's life. Fabian Escalante, once tasked with Castro's protection, contends that there were 638 assassination attempts. Whatever the true figure is, Escalante would appear to have been better at his job than the entire CIA was at theirs.

A young man who does not have what it takes to perform military service is not likely to have what it takes to make a living.

No one has been barred on account of his
race from fighting or dying for America,
there are no 'white' or 'coloured' signs on
the foxholes or graveyards of battle.

Those who make peaceful revolution impossible
will make violent revolution inevitable.

GEORGE KENNEY

(1889–1977, AMERICAN AIR FORCE COMMANDER)

Air power is like poker. A second-best hand is like none
at all – it will cost you dough and win you nothing.

BRUCE KENT

(BORN 1929, BRITISH POLITICAL ACTIVIST)

War is as barbaric a means of resolving
conflict as cannibalism is as a means
of coping with diet deficiencies.

ELLEN KEY

(1849–1926, SWEDISH WRITER)

Everything, everything in war is barbaric... But
the worst barbarity of war is that it forces men
collectively to commit acts against which individually
they would revolt with their whole being.

GENGHIS KHAN

(C. 1162–1227, MONGOLIAN EMPEROR)

The greatest happiness is to vanquish your enemies,
to chase them before you, to rob them of their
wealth, to see those dear to them bathed in tears, to
clasp to your bosom their wives and daughters.

It is not sufficient that I succeed – all others must fail.

I am the Flail of God… If you had not
committed great sins, God would not have
sent a punishment like me upon you.

All who surrender will be spared; whoever
does not surrender but opposes with struggle
and dissension, shall be annihilated.

*During the Mongol Empire's war with Khwarezm (present-
day Uzbekistan, Kazakhstan and Turkmenistan)*

Those who were adept and brave fellows I
have made military commanders. Those who
were quick and nimble I have made herders of
horses. Those who were not adept I have given
a small whip and sent to be shepherds.

With Heaven's aid I have conquered for you a huge
empire. But my life was too short to achieve the
conquest of the world. That task is left for you.

To his sons at the end of his life

MOHAMMED DAOUD KHAN

(1909–1978, AFGHAN PRESIDENT)

I feel the happiest when I can light my
American cigarettes with Soviet matches.

ARUN KHETARPAL

(1950–1971, INDIAN ARMY OFFICER)

No Sir, I will not abandon my tank.
My gun is still working.

Just before he was fatally wounded during the Bangladesh War

NIKITA KHRUSHCHEV

(1894–1971, SOVIET LEADER)

The more bombers, the less room for doves of peace.

Bombs do not choose. They will hit everything.

Support by United States rulers is rather in the nature
of the support that the rope gives to a hanged man.

KIM JONG-IL

(1942–2011, SUPREME LEADER OF NORTH KOREA)

A man who dreads trials and difficulties
cannot become a revolutionary.

THEY SHALL NOT PASS!

ALTHOUGH WOUNDED AND IN a burning tank during the Bangladesh War of 1971, twenty-one-year-old Arun Khetarpal of the 17th Poona Horse fought on until he was killed, for which he was posthumously awarded the Param Vir Chakra, the Indian Army's highest award for 'valour or self-sacrifice in the presence of the enemy' (it replaced the Victoria Cross shortly after India gained its independence in 1947). He had attacked Pakistani positions relentlessly and had taken out five enemy tanks before being hit for a second time. The Pakistanis were denied the breakthrough they had fought so hard for. Within twenty-four hours the war was over. Arun Khetarpal's mother celebrated along with everybody else and cleaned up her son's room and motorcycle while she waited for him to come home. It was to be another week before she learned the news.

The Pakistani commander responsible for hitting Khetarpal's tank, Khwaja Mohammad Naser, was so impressed with the bravery of his opposite number that he enquired about him after the battle, only to be told that he had been killed. Many years later, upon meeting Khetarpal's father, he described the young tank commander as 'standing like an insurmountable rock between victory and failure.'

Today, in a fitting tribute to him, cadets at the Indian Military Academy pass out as officers through the Khetarpal Building.

MARTIN LUTHER KING JR

(1929–1968, AMERICAN CIVIL RIGHTS ACTIVIST)

A nation that continues year after year to spend
more money on military defence than on programs
of social uplift is approaching spiritual doom.

War is a poor chisel to carve out tomorrow.

The chain reaction of evil – hate begetting hate,
wars producing more wars – must be broken.

We can never forget that everything
Hitler did in Germany was 'legal'.

RUDYARD KIPLING

(1865–1936, ENGLISH WRITER)

He became an officer and a gentleman,
which is an enviable thing.
Only a Subaltern

The snow lies thick on Valley Forge,
The ice on the Delaware,
But the poor dead soldiers of King George,
They neither know nor care.
They will not stir when the drifts are gone,
Or the ice melts out of the bay:
And the men that served Washington
Lie all as still as they.
From 'The American Rebellion'

Faithless the watch that I kept:
now I have none to keep.
I was slain because I slept: now I am slain I sleep.
Let no man reproach me again;
whatever watch is unkept –
I sleep because I am slain. They slew me because I slept.

From the World War One poem 'The Sleepy Sentinel'

Tho' I've belted you and flayed you,

By the livin' Gawd that made you,
You're a better man than I am, Gunga Din!

*From 'Gunga Din', a poem about an Indian native
who dies saving the life of a British soldier.*

JEANE KIRKPATRICK

(1926–2006, FIRST FEMALE AMERICAN AMBASSADOR TO THE UN)

Straying off course is not recognised as a
capital crime by civilised nations.

Referring to the Soviet destruction of Korean Air flight 007 in 1983

We have war when at least one of the parties to a
conflict wants something more than it wants peace.

HENRY KISSINGER

(BORN 1923, GERMAN-AMERICAN WRITER
AND US SECRETARY OF STATE)

No country can act wisely simultaneously in every
part of the globe at every moment of time.

The task of the leader is to get his people from
where they are to where they have not been.

No one will ever win the battle of the sexes;
there's too much fraternising with the enemy.

The guerrilla wins if he does not lose. The
conventional army loses if it does not win.

The superpowers often behave like two heavily
armed blind men feeling their way around a room,
each believing himself in mortal peril from the
other, whom he assumes to have perfect vision.

*Referring to the tension of the cold war
that followed World War Two*

Hendrik Klopper

(1902–1978, South African military commander)

Am sending mobile troops out tonight.
Not possible to hold tomorrow… Will
resist to the last man and last round.

Whilst in charge of the Tobruk Garrison in 1942

Arthur Koestler

(1905–1983, Hungarian-British writer)

The most persistent sound that reverberates through
man's history is the beating of war drums.

KARL KRAUS

(1874–1936, AUSTRIAN WRITER)

War is, at first, the hope that one will be better off; next, the expectation that the other fellow will be worse off; then, the satisfaction that he isn't any better off; and, finally, the surprise at everyone's being worse off.

AUNG SAN SUU KYI

(BORN 1945, BURMESE OPPOSITION LEADER)

Peace as a goal is an ideal which will not be contested by any government or nation, not even the most belligerent.

L

Lao Tzu

(SIXTH CENTURY BC, CHINESE PHILOSOPHER)

He who knows others is wise. He who knows himself
is enlightened. He who conquers others has physical
strength. He who conquers himself is strong.

Tao Te Ching

T. E. Lawrence

(OF ARABIA) (1888–1935, BRITISH ARMY OFFICER)

Nine-tenths of tactics are certain, and taught in books:
but the irrational tenth is like the kingfisher flashing
across the pool, and that is the test of generals.

The printing press is the greatest weapon in
the armoury of the modern commander.

DO THESE COME IN 'EXTRA SMALL'?

IT HAS BEEN SAID that when Lawrence tried to join up in 1914 he was refused for failing to meet the height requirement, and that the army only gave in when it realised how well suited he was to intelligence work in Cairo, on account of the years he had already spent in the Middle East as an archaeologist, achieving fluent Arabic in the process.

He played an active role once the Arab Revolt against Turkish rule broke out in 1916, but what stood him apart from other British officers engaged in support of the Arabs was his ability to think and speak like them, his willingness to behave and dress and eat in their traditional ways, and his strong conviction that it was their war, not his. Living amongst them, he gained their respect and they enjoyed the benefits of his tactical brilliance, particularly when it came to guerrilla warfare. Victory after victory ensued against the far superior forces of the Kaiser-backed Ottoman Empire.

He was to emerge from the war a lone, enigmatic figure, framed heroically against the vast desert sands. Lawrence of Arabia was to be immortalised and not even his own account of the horrors and deprivations of that war (in his book, *Seven Pillars of Wisdom*) could slow the romantic bandwagon. And neither could the fact that he had always had to order those trademark Arab robes in 'extra small'.

To me an unnecessary action, or shot, or casualty, was not only waste but sin.

Do not try to do too much with your own hands. Better the Arabs do it tolerably than that you do it perfectly. It is their war, and you are to help them, not to win it for them.

From a guide Lawrence wrote for British officers in 1917

GUSTAVE LE BON

(1841–1931, FRENCH PSYCHOLOGIST)

War reveals to a people its weaknesses, but also its virtues.

STANISŁAW JERZY LEC

(1909–1966, POLISH POET)

In a war of ideas, it is people who get killed.

ROBERT E. LEE

(1807–1870, AMERICAN CONFEDERATE ARMY GENERAL)

It is well that war is horrible, otherwise we should grow too fond of it.

Do your duty in all things. You cannot do more. You should never wish to do less.

I have been up to see the Congress and they do not seem to be able to do anything except to eat peanuts and chew tobacco, while my army is starving.

What a cruel thing war is to fill our hearts with hatred instead of love for our neighbours.

We must expect reverses, even defeats. They are sent to teach us wisdom and prudence, to call forth greater energies, and to prevent our falling into greater disasters.

We have fought this fight as long, and as well as we know how. We have been defeated. For us as a Christian people, there is now but one course to pursue. We must accept the situation.

VLADIMIR LENIN

(1870–1924, RUSSIAN MARXIST REVOLUTIONARY)

The capitalists will sell us the rope with which we will hang them.

Can a nation be free if it oppresses other nations? It cannot.

It is impossible to predict the time and progress of revolution. It is governed by its own more or less mysterious laws.

One of the basic conditions for the victory of socialism is the arming of the workers and the disarming of the bourgeoisie.

Only an armed people can be the real bulwark of popular liberty.

JEAN-PIERRE LÉVY

(1911–1996, FRENCH RESISTANCE LEADER)

We lived in the shadows as soldiers of the night…
tragedy awaited all of us just around the corner.

ABRAHAM LINCOLN

(1809–1865, SIXTEENTH PRESIDENT OF THE UNITED STATES)

The probability that we may fail in the
struggle ought not to deter us from the
support of a cause we believe to be just.

You can have anything you want – if you want
it badly enough. You can be anything you want
to be, have anything you desire, accomplish
anything you set out to accomplish – if you will
hold to that desire with singleness of purpose.

Force is all-conquering, but its victories are short-lived.

I can make more generals, but horses cost money.

I destroy my enemies when I make them my friends.

Those who deny freedom to others
deserve it not for themselves.

Avoid popularity if you would have peace.

Dear Madam,

I have been shown in the files of the War Department a statement of the Adjutant General of Massachusetts that you are the mother of five sons who have died gloriously on the field of battle. I feel how weak and fruitless must be any word of mine which should attempt to beguile you from the grief of a loss so overwhelming. But I cannot refrain from tendering you the consolation that may be found in the thanks of the Republic they died to save. I pray that our Heavenly Father may assuage the anguish of your bereavement, and leave you only the cherished memory of the loved and lost, and the solemn pride that must be yours to have laid so costly a sacrifice upon the altar of freedom.

Yours, very sincerely and respectfully,

A. Lincoln
Letter written to Mrs Lydia Bixby, dated 21 November 1864

CHARLES LINDBERGH

(1902–1974, AMERICAN AVIATION PIONEER)

I have seen the science I worshipped, and the aircraft I loved, destroying the civilisation I expected them to serve.
Of Flight and Life

FRANZ LISZT

(1811–1886, HUNGARIAN COMPOSER)

I am not fond of speaking about politics
because I don't have in my possession
an army of 200,000 soldiers.

LIVY

(59 BC–AD 17, ROMAN HISTORIAN)

Vae victis. (Woe to the vanquished.)

The study of history is the best medicine for a
sick mind; for in history you have a record of
the infinite variety of human experience plainly
set out for all to see: and in that record you can
find for yourself and your country both examples
and warnings: fine things to take as models; base
things, rotten through and through, to avoid.

HENRY WADSWORTH LONGFELLOW

(1807–1882, AMERICAN POET)

If we could read the secret history of our enemies
we should find in each man's life sorrow and
suffering enough to disarm all hostility.

A Lady with a Lamp shall stand
In the great history of the land,
A noble type of good,
Heroic womanhood.

From 'Santa Filomena', 1857 (reference is to
Florence Nightingale in the Crimean War)

ANDREA DE LOO

(SIXTEENTH CENTURY, SPANISH AMBASSADOR
TO THE COURT OF ELIZABETH I)

Your Majesty will not hear words, so
we must come to the cannon.

CLAUDE LOUIS

(1707–1778, FRENCH GENERAL AND COMTE DE SAINT-GERMAIN)

An army must inevitably consist of the scum of the
people and all those for which society has no use.

DAVID LOW

(1891–1963, NEW ZEALAND POLITICAL CARTOONIST)

To draw a hostile warlord as a horrible
monster is to play his game. What he doesn't
like is being shown as a silly ass.

JAMES M. LOWE

(TWENTY-FIRST CENTURY, UNITED STATES MARINE)

I like Marines, because being a Marine is a serious business. We're not a social club or a fraternal organisation and we don't pretend to be one. We're a brotherhood of warriors – nothing more, nothing less, pure and simple. We are in the ass-kicking business and, unfortunately, these days business is good.

Speaking in 2004

LUCAN

(AD 39–65, ROMAN POET)

Deep are the wounds that civil strife inflicts.

Great fear is concealed under daring.

LUCRETIUS

(C. 99–55 BC, ROMAN POET)

Pleasant it [be] to behold great encounters of warfare arrayed over the plains, with no part of yours in peril.

MARTIN LUTHER

(1483–1546, GERMAN PROTESTANT REFORMER)

War is the greatest plague that can afflict humanity,
it destroys religion, it destroys states, it destroys
families. Any scourge is preferable to it.

LYCURGUS

(C. 820–730 BC, SPARTAN REFORMER AND LAWGIVER)

To brave men, the prizes that war
offers are liberty and fame.

M

MA YUAN

(14 BC–AD 49, CHINESE GENERAL)

A real man dies on a battlefield, and his body is wrapped in horsehide. Who wants to die in bed, surrounded by his wife and children?

DOUGLAS MACARTHUR

(1880–1964, AMERICAN ARMY GENERAL)

In no other profession are the penalties for employing untrained personnel so appalling or so irrevocable as in the military.

I have known war as few men now living know it... Its very destructiveness on both friend and foe has rendered it useless as a means of settling international disputes.

In war, you win or lose, live or die – and
the difference is just an eyelash.

We are not retreating – we are
advancing in another direction.

NICCOLÒ MACHIAVELLI

(1469–1527, ITALIAN HISTORIAN AND PHILOSOPHER)

A battle that you win cancels all your mistakes.

If one wishes to be obeyed, it is necessary
to know how to command.

Hence it comes that all armed Prophets
have been victorious, and all unarmed
Prophets have been destroyed.

Never do an enemy a small injury.

No enterprise is more likely to succeed than one
concealed from the enemy until it is ripe for execution.

There is no avoiding war; it can only be
postponed to the advantage of others.

ALFRED THAYER MAHAN

(1840–1914, AMERICAN NAVAL OFFICER AND HISTORIAN)

The study of history lies at the foundation of
all sound military conclusions and practice.

Organised force alone enables the quiet and the weak
to go about their business and to sleep securely in
their beds, safe from the violent without or within.

THOMAS DE MAHY

(1744–1790, FRENCH ARISTOCRAT)

I see that you have made three spelling mistakes.

*Upon reading his death sentence before being hanged for plotting
to help Louis XVI and Marie Antoinette escape the country*

HORACE MANN

(1796–1859, AMERICAN REFORMER)

Be ashamed to die until you have won
some victory for humanity.

Do not think of knocking out another person's
brains because he differs in opinion from you. It
would be as rational to knock yourself on the head
because you differ from yourself ten years ago.

THOMAS MANN

(1875–1955, GERMAN WRITER AND PHILANTHROPIST)

War is a cowardly escape from the problems of peace.

Reduced to a miserable mass level, the
level of a Hitler, German Romanticism
broke out into hysterical barbarism.

MAO ZEDONG

(1893–1976, CHINESE REVOLUTIONARY LEADER)

War can only be abolished through war... in order to get rid of the gun it is necessary to take up the gun.

An army without culture is a dull-witted army, and a dull-witted army cannot defeat the enemy.

The guerrilla must move amongst the people as a fish swims in the sea.

Political power grows out of the barrel of a gun.

Politics is war without bloodshed while war is politics with bloodshed.

GEORGE C. MARSHALL

(1880–1959, US SECRETARY OF DEFENSE)

Unless the soldier's soul sustains him, he cannot be relied on and will fail himself and his country in the end.

There is no limit to the good you can do if you don't care who gets the credit.

GROUCHO MARX

(1890–1977, AMERICAN COMEDIAN)

Military intelligence is a contradiction in terms.

Military justice is to justice what
military music is to music.

DONALD F. MASON

(TWENTIETH CENTURY, AMERICAN NAVAL PILOT AND LIEUTENANT)

Sighted sub, sank same.

Report from United States Navy anti-submarine patrol in 1942

JOHN MASTERS

(1914–1983, ENGLISH WRITER AND OFFICER
IN THE BRITISH INDIAN ARMY)

Nothing raises morale better than a dead general.

The Road Past Mandalay

If you feel entirely comfortable, then you're
not far enough ahead to do any good.

GUY DE MAUPASSANT

(1850–1893, FRENCH WRITER)

Every government has as much of a duty to avoid
war as a ship's captain has to avoid a shipwreck.

Patriotism is a kind of religion; it is the
egg from which wars are hatched.

My Uncle Sosthenes

Military men are the scourges of the world.

GIUSEPPE MAZZINI

(1805–1872, ITALIAN REVOLUTIONARY)

Insurrection by means of guerrilla bands is the true method of warfare for all nations desirous of emancipating themselves from a foreign yoke. It is invincible, indestructible.

So long as you are ready to die for humanity, the life of your country is immortal.

JOHN MCCAIN

(BORN 1936, AMERICAN SENATOR)

War is wretched beyond description, and only a fool or a fraud could sentimentalise its cruel reality.

However just the cause, we should mourn for all that is lost when war claims its wages from us.

COLMAN MCCARTHY

(BORN 1938, AMERICAN JOURNALIST AND PEACE ACTIVIST)

Everyone's a pacifist between wars. It's like being a vegetarian between meals.

JOHN ALEXANDER McCRAE

(1872–1918, CANADIAN SOLDIER, PHYSICIAN AND POET)

We are the Dead. Short days ago
We lived, felt dawn, saw sunset glow,
Loved, and were loved, and now we lie
In Flanders fields.
Take up our quarrel with the foe:
To you from failing hands, we throw
The torch; be yours to hold it high.
If ye break faith with us who die
We shall not sleep, though poppies grow
In Flanders fields.

From 'In Flanders Fields'

GOLDA MEIR

(1898–1978, ISRAELI PRIME MINISTER)

It is true we have won all our wars, but we have
paid for them. We don't want victories anymore.

A leader who doesn't hesitate before he sends
his nation into battle is not fit to be a leader.

H. L. MENCKEN

(1880–1956, AMERICAN JOURNALIST AND WRITER)

War will never cease until babies begin to
come into the world with larger cerebrums
and smaller adrenal glands.

I believe in only one thing: liberty; but I do not believe
in liberty enough to want to force it upon anyone.

In war the heroes always outnumber
the soldiers ten to one.

It doesn't take a majority to make a rebellion; it takes
only a few determined leaders and a sound cause.

The urge to save humanity is almost always
a false front for the urge to rule.

GEORGE MEREDITH

(1828–1909, ENGLISH WRITER)

For he is Britain's Admiral,
Till the setting of her sun.
Referring to Horatio Nelson in 'Trafalgar Day'

EVE MERRIAM

(1916–1992, AMERICAN WRITER)

I dream of giving birth to a child who
will ask, 'Mother, what was war?'

JOHN STUART MILL

(1806–1873, BRITISH PHILOSOPHER)

War is an ugly thing but not the ugliest of things: the
decayed and degraded state of moral and patriotic

feelings which thinks that nothing is worth war is much worse... A man who has nothing for which he is willing to fight, nothing which is more important than his own personal safety, is a miserable creature and has no chance of being free unless made and kept so by the exertions of better men than himself.

THE MANY LIVES OF LEE MILLER

By the time Lee Miller left London in 1944 to cover the remainder of the war as the only female reporter in the combat zone, she had been a top model for Vogue in New York, spent time in Paris with Surrealist artist and photographer Man Ray, lived in Cairo with her first husband, and moved to London with her future second husband, Roland Penrose, another Surrealist artist. She had established herself as a first-class fashion and fine art photographer in both London and Paris, and had been covering the London Blitz for Vogue to boot. The transformation she made from being the centre of attention in an exclusive world of art to that of a war correspondent on the front line was nothing short of staggering. She witnessed at close quarters the siege of St Malo, the liberation of Paris and the concentration camps at Buchenwald and Dachau. She billeted in Hitler's vacated house in Munich (even making use of his bath), and photographed his house at Berchtesgaden in flames on the eve of Germany's surrender. She moved east to cover the harrowing scenes of children dying of starvation in Vienna and the execution of Hungarian prime minister Lázló Bárdossy. When you take account of the conditions she was working under, and the fact that she didn't have the best of equipment, the quality of her photography was astonishing.

LEE MILLER

(1907–1977, AMERICAN PHOTOGRAPHER AND WAR REPORTER)

I had thought that watching a battle
from a hillside had gone out with the
glamorous paintings of Napoleon.

*In a cable reporting that she had a grandstand
view of the battle for St Malo, August 1944*

C. WRIGHT MILLS

(1916–1962, AMERICAN SOCIOLOGIST)

The principal cause of war is war itself.

JOHN MILTON

(1608–1674, ENGLISH POET)

Who overcomes by force, hath
overcome but half his foe.

CHARLES EDWARD MONTAGUE

(1867–1928, ENGLISH JOURNALIST AND WRITER)

War hath no fury like a non-combatant.

The number of medals on an officer's breast
varies in inverse proportion to the square of the
distance of his duties from the front line.

BERNARD MONTGOMERY OF ALAMEIN

(1887–1976, BRITISH ARMY COMMANDER)

The beginning of leadership is a battle
for the hearts and minds of men.

It is always a good thing to persuade the soldier
that what you want him to do is right.

The morale of the soldier is the greatest single
factor in war and the best way to achieve a high
morale in wartime is by success in battle.

There is far too much paper in circulation in the army,
and no one can read even half of it intelligently.

The commander must decide how he will fight
the battle before it begins. He must then decide
how he will use the military effort at his disposal
to force the battle to swing the way he wishes
it to go; he must make the enemy dance to his
tune from the beginning and not vice versa.

Discipline strengthens the mind so that it becomes
impervious to the corroding influence of fear.

Every soldier must know, before he goes into
battle, how the little battle he is to fight fits into
the larger picture, and how the success of his
fighting will influence the battle as a whole.

I have cancelled the plan for withdrawal. If we are attacked, then there will be no retreat. If we cannot stay here alive, then we will stay here dead.

To his officers at the first meeting he held with them in the North African desert in 1942, having just assumed control of the Eighth Army

OUTFOXED BY RATS

MONTGOMERY'S ARRIVAL IN THE North African desert in August 1942 transformed the morale and fighting ability of the British Eighth Army. Everybody knew that he had form, having already served in Ireland, Palestine, Egypt, India, Belgium and France, and all of that since being seriously wounded in the trenches of World War One. He set about securing reinforcements, coordinating the efforts of the army with those of the air force and the navy and personally visiting every unit that was going to be fighting under him, including the Australian, Indian, South African, New Zealand, Greek and Free French ones. His first decisive victory was won at El Alamein two months later and the tide of battle against Rommel's Afrikakorps had turned. A combination of brilliant tactics, clear-cut orders and excellent morale (sickness and absenteeism were said to have been virtually eliminated) brought about victory in North Africa by May the following year. Although Montgomery would enjoy further success in Sicily and Italy, and then during the invasion of Normandy and on to the Rhine, he will always be chiefly remembered for galvanising the 'Desert Rats' of the Eighth Army into bringing down the 'Desert Fox' that Hitler had sent to hunt them down.

HAL MOORE

(BORN 1922, AMERICAN ARMY LIEUTENANT GENERAL)

American soldiers in battle don't fight for what some president says on TV, they don't fight for mom, apple pie, the American flag… they fight for one another.

JAMES K. MORROW

(BORN 1947, AMERICAN WRITER)

'There are no atheists in foxholes' isn't an argument against atheism, it's an argument against foxholes.

T. MICHAEL MOSELEY

(BORN 1949, AMERICAN AIR FORCE GENERAL)

I find it interesting when folks say we're softening them up. We're not softening them up, we're killing them.

Referring to the Republican Guard divisions outside of Baghdad, 5 April 2003

DICK MOTTA

(BORN 1931, AMERICAN BASKETBALL COACH)

War is the only game in which it doesn't pay to have home-court advantage.

MIYAMOTO MUSASHI

(1584–1645, JAPANESE KENSEI WARRIOR AND STRATEGIST)

Generally speaking, the Way of the warrior
is resolute acceptance of death.

Strategy is the craft of the warrior. Commanders must
enact the craft, and troopers should know this Way.

This is a truth: when you sacrifice your life, you must
make fullest use of your weaponry. It is false not
to do so, and to die with a weapon yet undrawn.

Both in fighting and in everyday life you
should be determined though calm. Meet
the situation without tenseness yet not
recklessly, your spirit settled yet unbiased.

If the enemy thinks of the mountains,
attack like the sea; and if he thinks of
the sea, attack like the mountains.

BENITO MUSSOLINI

(1883–1945, ITALIAN FASCIST DICTATOR)

It is humiliating to remain with our hands folded
while others write history. It matters little who wins.

It is better to live one day as a lion than
one hundred years as a sheep.

Blood alone moves the wheels of history.

A nation of spaghetti eaters cannot
restore Roman civilisation!

War alone... imposes the stamp of nobility upon
the peoples who have the courage to make it.

N

NABESHIMA NAOSHIGE

(1537–1619, JAPANESE WARLORD)

No matter whether a person belongs to the upper
or lower ranks, if he has not put his life on the
line at least once he has cause for shame.

NĀGĀRJUNA

(C. AD 150–250, BUDDHIST TEACHER)

Although you may spend your life killing, you
will not exhaust all your foes. But if you quell
your own anger, your real enemy will be slain.

JOSÉ NAROSKY

(BORN 1930, ARGENTINIAN WRITER)

In war, there are no unwounded soldiers.

GAMAL ABDEL NASSER

(1918–1970, EGYPTIAN PRESIDENT AND ARMY COMMANDER)

What was taken by force, can
only be restored by force.

There is no longer a way out of our present
situation except by forging a road toward our
objective, violently and by force, over a sea of
blood and under a horizon blazing with fire.

We have to go along a road covered with blood. We
have no other alternative. For us it is a matter of
life or death, a matter of living or existing. We have
to be ready to face the challenges that await us.

People do not want words – they want the
sound of battle – the battle of destiny.

HOLLY NEAR

(BORN 1949, AMERICAN SINGER AND ACTIVIST)

Why do we kill people who are killing people
to show that killing people is wrong?

JAWAHARLAL NEHRU

(1889–1964, INDIAN LEADER)

It is the habit of every aggressor nation to
claim that it is acting on the defensive.

Without peace, all other dreams vanish
and are reduced to ashes.

Peace is not merely the absence of war.
It is also a state of mind. Lasting peace
can come only to peaceful people.

At the stroke of the midnight hour, when the world
sleeps, India will awake to life and freedom.
At the end of India's long struggle for independence, August 1947

HORATIO NELSON

(1758–1805, BRITISH NAVAL COMMANDER)

You must consider every man your enemy who
speaks ill of your King, and you must treat every
Frenchman as if he were the Devil himself.

Before this time tomorrow I shall have
gained a Peerage or Westminster Abbey.
Before the Battle of the Nile, 1798

My brave officers… Such a gallant set
of fellows! Such a band of brothers! My
heart swells at the thought of them!

If I had been censured every time I have run my
ship, or fleets under my command, into great
danger, I should have long ago been out of the
Service and never in the House of Peers.

I cannot, if I am in the field of glory, be kept out
of sight: wherever there is anything to be done,
there Providence is sure to direct my steps.

My greatest happiness is to serve my gracious King and
Country and I am envious only of glory; for if it be a
sin to covet glory I am the most offending soul alive.

Duty is the great business of a sea officer;
all private considerations must give way
to it, however painful it may be.

I have only one eye; I have a right to be blind
sometimes... I really do not see the signal!

*This was reportedly Nelson's response to a flagged signal
from Admiral Sir Hyde Parker to disengage at the Battle of
Copenhagen in 1801. Nelson went on to take Copenhagen.*

It is warm work; and this day may be the last
to any of us at a moment. But mark you! I
would not be elsewhere for thousands.

At the Battle of Copenhagen, 1801

England expects that every man will do his duty.

Before the Battle of Trafalgar, 1805

My seamen are now what British seamen
ought to be... almost invincible; they
really mind shot no more than peas.

AS TOUGH AS OLD BOOTS

AS WE ALL KNOW, Nelson suffered more than his fair share of significant battle wounds. He was blinded in the right eye early on in his career, during the siege of Calvi in 1794. The ship's surgeon had to amputate his dangling right forearm after it was shot through off Santa Cruz in 1797, although within half an hour he was again issuing instructions to his captains. The musket wound that was to prove fatal in 1805 was suffered on board HMS Victory at the Battle of Trafalgar, but even then it took three and a half hours for the wound to kill him.

It is also well documented that Nelson had to overcome, on a regular basis, seasickness, toothache, dysentery, malaria, gout, palpitations and breathlessness. You could almost be forgiven for thinking that this was a man who was not cut out for a life at sea in the first place, but they probably couldn't find a medical officer brave enough to tell him that!

Our country will, I believe, sooner forgive an officer for attacking an enemy than for letting it alone.

No captain can do very wrong if he puts his ship alongside that of the enemy.

I hate your pen-and-ink men; a fleet of British ships of war are the best negotiators in Europe.

Letter to Lady Emma Hamilton, 1801

Let me alone: I have yet my legs and one arm. Tell the surgeon to make haste with his instruments. I know I must lose my right arm; so the sooner it's off the better.

*After being wounded during the attack on
Santa Cruz de Tenerife in 1797*

Thank God I have done my duty.

While dying from a musket bullet at Trafalgar

MARTIN NIEMÖLLER

(1892–1984, GERMAN PASTOR)

First they came for the communists, and I didn't speak out because I wasn't a communist.

Then they came for the trade unionists, and I didn't speak out because I wasn't a trade unionist.

Then they came for the Jews, and I didn't speak out because I wasn't a Jew.

Then they came for me and there was no one left to speak out for me.

*On the inactivity of German intellectuals
at the time of the Nazi purges*

FRIEDRICH NIETZSCHE

(1844–1900, GERMAN PHILOSOPHER)

He who fights with monsters might take care lest he thereby become a monster. And if you gaze for long into an abyss, the abyss gazes also into you.

The best weapon against an enemy is another enemy.

What does not kill me makes me stronger.

War has always been the grand sagacity of every spirit
that has grown too inward and too profound; its
curative power lies even in the wounds one receives.

If one would have a friend, then must one also be
willing to wage war for him: and in order to wage
war, one must be capable of being an enemy.

How good bad music and bad reasons sound
when we march against an enemy.

FLORENCE NIGHTINGALE
(1820–1910, ENGLISH NURSING PIONEER)

I can stand out the war with any man.

I stand at the altar of the murdered men,
and, while I live, I fight their cause.

It may seem a strange principle to enunciate
as the very first requirement in a hospital
that it should do the sick no harm.

KWAME NKRUMAH
(1909–1972, FIRST PRESIDENT OF GHANA)

Revolutions are brought about by men, by men who
think as men of action and act as men of thought.

Freedom is not something that one people can
bestow on another as a gift. They claim it as
their own and none can keep it from them.

FROM RICHES TO
DISEASE-RIDDEN RAGS

FLORENCE NIGHTINGALE COULD HAVE enjoyed the
good life. She was born into comfort and received
first-class education, at home and abroad, from her
father and governesses. A good marriage, travels
abroad and a well-connected place in society
were hers for the taking. But, by the time she was
seventeen, she heard the voice of God telling her
that she had a more important mission in life, and
so, against her parents' wishes, she opted for the
rather unrespectable profession of nursing.

Responding to the plight of wounded British
servicemen in the military hospitals of the Crimea in
1854, she found herself confronted with appalling
conditions and a hopelessly high mortality rate.
She set about methodical analysis of the causes
and effects and ultimately effected improvements
to logistics, sanitation and the control of disease
and infection. She was able to request funding
and supplies from home with hitherto unheard of
speed thanks to the advent of the telegraph.

However, it was mostly her (lamp-lit) bedside
manner that was making her famous back home,
and she was a heroine by the time she returned,
but she shunned all the attention in order to carry
on with her groundbreaking medical and social
reforms, which she did until she was well into her
old age.

O

BARACK OBAMA

(BORN 1961, FORTY-FOURTH PRESIDENT OF THE UNITED STATES)

The war does not end when you come home.
It lives on in memories of your fellow soldiers,
sailors, airmen and Marines who gave their
lives. It endures in the wound that is slow to
heal, the disability that isn't going away.

From his address to troops at Camp Lejeune, 2009

For we know that our patchwork heritage is a
strength, not a weakness... We are shaped by every
language and culture, drawn from every end of this
Earth; and because we have tasted the bitter swill
of civil war and segregation... we cannot help but
believe that the old hatreds shall some day pass.

Excerpt from his inaugural address, 20 January 2009

I don't oppose all wars. What I am opposed to is a
dumb war. What I am opposed to is a rash war.

Where the stakes are the highest, in the war
on terror, we cannot possibly succeed without
extraordinary international cooperation.

KENZABURŌ ŌE

(BORN 1935, JAPANESE WRITER)

After the end of the Second World War
it was a categorical imperative for us to
declare that we renounced war forever in a
central article of the new Constitution.

The Japanese chose the principle of eternal peace as
the basis of morality for our rebirth after the war.

BERNARDO O'HIGGINS

(1778–1842, CHILEAN INDEPENDENCE LEADER)

Those who can ride, ride! We will
break through the enemy!
On breaking away from the lost Battle of Rancagua in 1814

Live with honour or die with glory!
He who is brave, follow me!
At a crucial point in the Battle of El Roble in 1813

163

AND THE TOP OF THE
MAÑANA TO YOU TOO

BERNARDO O'HIGGINS WAS THE son of Ambrosio (born Ambrose) O'Higgins; an Irish engineer from County Sligo who impressively worked his way up to become Spanish colonial captain general of Chile and viceroy of Peru. While studying in Spain, Bernardo was exposed to many South American liberation leaders and when Napoleon invaded Spain in 1808, he took this as a cue to begin fighting for Chilean independence.

He was an unlikely revolutionary hero, with an even more unlikely name. He was not an especially brilliant strategist or commander, and he lacked the charisma of a Simón Bolívar. But he was brave, honest and dedicated to the cause of liberty. When he took command at a crucial point in the Battle of El Noble in 1813, he secured an important victory and got himself promoted to commander-in-chief of the army. By 1818 the Spanish Royalist forces had been defeated and O'Higgins became the first leader of his liberated country. His ensuing five-year rule as virtual dictator has been considered harsh but fair and in any event his failings have long since been forgiven by the Chilean people, who have named an entire region after him, as well as several navy ships, a military base, a park, a lake, countless streets and a bank. Unfortunately, the brilliantly named Banco O'Higgins is no more, having become part of Banco Santiago in 1997.

ROBIN OLDS

(1922–2007, AMERICAN AIR FORCE PILOT AND GENERAL)

Anybody who doesn't have fear is an idiot. It's
just that you must make the fear work for you.

GEORGE ORWELL

(1903–1950, ENGLISH WRITER AND JOURNALIST)

Men can only be highly civilised while
other men, inevitably less civilised, are
there to guard and feed them.

The quickest way of ending a war is to lose it.

To walk through the ruined cities of Germany is to feel
an actual doubt about the continuity of civilisation.

Probably the Battle of Waterloo was won on the
playing fields of Eton, but the opening battles
of all subsequent wars have been lost there.

The essential act of war is destruction, not necessarily
of human lives, but of the products of human labour.

War against a foreign country only happens when the
moneyed classes think they are going to profit from it.

All the war propaganda, all the screaming
and lies and hatred, comes invariably
from people who are not fighting.

War is evil, but it is often the lesser evil.

To survive it is often necessary to fight and
to fight you have to dirty yourself.

Every war… is represented not as a war but as an
act of self-defence against a homicidal maniac.

As I write, highly civilised human beings
are flying overhead, trying to kill me.

WILFRED OWEN

(1893–1918, ENGLISH SOLDIER AND POET)

This book is not about heroes. English
Poetry is not yet fit to speak of them.

Nor is it about deeds, or lands, nor anything
about glory, honour, might, majesty,
dominion, or power, except War.

Above all I am not concerned with Poetry.

My subject is War, and the pity of War.
From a preface to a planned book of his poetry

If I have got to be a soldier, I must be a
good one, anything else is unthinkable.

Do you know what would hold me together on a
battlefield? The sense that I was perpetuating the
language in which Keats and the rest of them wrote!

In all my dreams, before my helpless sight,
He plunges at me, guttering, choking, drowning.
If in some smothering dreams you too could pace
Behind the wagon that we flung him in,
And watch the white eyes writhing in his face,
His hanging face, like a devil's sick of sin;
If you could hear, at every jolt, the blood
Come gargling from the froth-corrupted lungs,
Obscene as cancer, bitter as the cud
Of vile, incurable sores on innocent tongues,–
My friend, you would not tell with such high zest
To children ardent for some desperate glory,
The old Lie; Dulce et decorum est
Pro patria mori.

From 'Dulce et Decorum est'

P

THOMAS PAINE

(1737–1809, ANGLO-AMERICAN WRITER AND POLITICAL ACTIVIST)

The harder the conflict, the more glorious the triumph.

The cunning of the fox is as murderous
as the violence of the wolf.

An army of principles can penetrate
where an army of soldiers cannot.

Arms discourage and keep the invader and plunderer
in awe, and preserve order in the world as well
as property... Horrid mischief would ensue were
the law-abiding deprived of the use of them.

He who is the author of a war lets loose
the whole contagion of hell and opens a
vein that bleeds a nation to death.

It is not a field of a few acres of ground, but a cause, that we are defending, and whether we defeat the enemy in one battle, or by degrees, the consequences will be the same.

To establish any mode to abolish war, however advantageous it might be to Nations, would be to take from such Government the most lucrative of its branches.

War involves in its progress such a train of unforeseen circumstances that no human wisdom can calculate the end; it has but one thing certain, and that is to increase taxes.

If there must be trouble, let it be in my day, so that my children may have peace.

BLAISE PASCAL

(1623–1662, FRENCH POLYMATH)

Men never do evil so completely and cheerfully as when they do it from religious conviction.

Can anything be stupider than that a man has the right to kill me because he lives on the other side of a river and his ruler has a quarrel with mine, though I have not quarrelled with him?

HENRY JOHN 'HARRY' PATCH

(1898–2009, BRITISH SOLDIER)

If any man tells you he went into the front line and wasn't scared, he's a liar.

'THE LAST FIGHTING TOMMY'

AT THE TIME OF his death on 25 July 2009, aged 111 years 38 days, Harry Patch was the oldest man in Europe and the third-oldest man in the world. He was also the last surviving British soldier to have fought in the trenches of World War One. He fought in West Flanders (Belgium) for three months in 1917, until he was injured at the Battle of Passchendaele. On the occasion he came face to face with a German soldier who was rushing towards the Lewis gun that he was manning at the time, he could not bring himself to kill him, so he shot him in the shoulder. The German kept on coming, so he shot him above the knee and in the ankle, but he didn't kill him.

At the age of 106 he met up with Charles Kuentz, a 107-year-old veteran who had fought for the Germans at Passchendaele. Each declared the other to be a perfect gentleman and they exchanged gifts. Kuentz had brought along a tin of Alsatian biscuits and Patch a bottle of Somerset cider. As a tribute to Harry, the Gaymer Cider Company then produced 106 bottles of 'Patch's Pride Cider' for him and his friends to enjoy. Cheers, Harry!

Give your leaders each a gun and then
let them fight it out themselves.

Any one of them could have been me. Millions
of men came to fight in this war and I find
it incredible that I am the only one left.

*Commenting on graves at a Flanders war
cemetery in July 2007, at the age of 109*

GEORGE S. PATTON

(1885–1945, AMERICAN ARMY GENERAL)

Lead me, follow me, or get out of my way.

Courage is fear holding on a minute longer.

A good plan executed today is better than a perfect
plan executed at some indefinite point in the future.

Wars are not won by fighting battles;
wars are won by choosing battles.

A piece of spaghetti or a military unit
can only be led from the front end.

Have taken Trier with two Divisions. What
do you want me to do? Give it back?

*Reply to a message from Eisenhower to bypass the German city
of Trier because it would take four Divisions to capture it*

An army is a team. It lives, sleeps, eats and fights as a
team. This individual heroic stuff is pure horse shit.

From his speech to the Third Army, 1944

You name them; I'll shoot them.
Letter to Eisenhower, 1942

All men are timid on entering any fight;
whether it is the first or the last fight, all of
us are timid. Cowards are those who let their
timidity get the better of their manhood.
From a letter to his son, George, 1944

There's a great deal of talk about loyalty from the
bottom to the top. Loyalty from the top down is even
more necessary and is much less prevalent. One of the
most frequently noted characteristics of great men who
have remained great is loyalty to their subordinates.

There is only one tactical principle that is not subject
to change. It is to use the means at hand to inflict the
maximum amount of wound, death, and destruction
on the enemy in the minimum amount of time.

Live for something rather than die for nothing.

No good decision was ever made in a swivel chair.

I would rather have a German division in
front of me than a French one behind me.

JOHN PAUL II

(1920–2005, POLISH POPE)

Humanity should question itself, once more, about
the absurd and always unfair phenomenon of war.

War should belong to the tragic past,
to history: it should find no place on
humanity's agenda for the future.

The United Nations organisation has proclaimed 1979
as the Year of the Child. Are the children to receive
the arms race from us as a necessary inheritance?
Speaking at the UN in 1979

War is a defeat for humanity.

WILLIAM PENN

(1644–1718, AMERICAN COLONIST)

No man is fit to command another
that cannot command himself.

PERSIUS

(AD 34–62, ROMAN POET)

He conquers who endures.

PHAEDRUS

(C. 15 BC–AD 50, ROMAN FABLE-TELLER)

An alliance with the powerful is never to be trusted.

ARDANT DU PICQ

(1821–1870, FRENCH ARMY OFFICER)

The instruments of battle are valuable
only if one knows how to use them.

ALBERT PIKE

(1809–1891, AMERICAN CONFEDERATE OFFICER)

A war for a great principle ennobles a nation.

A man should live with his superiors as
he does with his fire: not too near, lest he
burn; nor too far off, lest he freeze.

PINDAR

(C. 522–443 BC, GREEK LYRIC POET)

Dulce bellum inexpertis. (War is sweet to
those who have never experienced it.)

The Latin version became well known after the Dutch
theologian, Erasmus, adopted it as the epigraph for
his meditation on the subject of war in 1515

WILLIAM PITT

(THE ELDER) (1708–1778, BRITISH PRIME MINISTER)

I am sure I can save this country, and nobody else can.

Upon the outbreak of the Seven Years' War in 1756

NOT THE LAST OF THE MOHICANS

THE SEVEN YEARS' WAR (1756–1763) was a global conflict that was played out across Europe, Africa, Asia and the Americas. The North American arm of the war was also known as the French and Indian War, which became the backdrop to James Fenimore Cooper's book *The Last of the Mohicans*, since popularised in the 1992 film of the same name.

Contrary to popular belief, however, the Mohican nation did not die out with Daniel Day Lewis. It is in fact alive and well today in the Stockbridge-Munsee Community in Wisconsin, although it cannot be said that the road to Wisconsin was an easy one. Starting with Henry Hudson on the Eastern Seaboard of the United States in 1609, British, Dutch and French settlers did their best to wipe out this proud Indian nation with everything they could muster – including warfare, disease, religious conversion and industrial-scale displacement. And it must have seemed rather ironic to the Mohicans who fought and died for the British in the Seven Years' War that one of the objectives of the conflict in that part of the world was to secure control of the territories that the British had only recently plundered from the Indians themselves!

If I were an American, as I am an Englishman, while a foreign troop was landed in my country, I would never lay down my arms – never – never – never!

WILLIAM PITT

(THE YOUNGER) (1759–1806, BRITISH PRIME MINISTER)

Most accursed, wicked, barbarous, cruel,
unnatural, unjust and diabolical.
On the American War of Independence

Roll up that map, it will not be wanted these ten years.
Upon seeing a map of Europe in January 1806, after hearing
of Napoleon's decisive victory at the Battle of Austerlitz

PLATO

(C. 424–347 BC, GREEK PHILOSOPHER)

Only the dead have seen the end of war.

Dictatorship naturally arises out of democracy,
and the most aggravated form of tyranny and
slavery out of the most extreme liberty.

When the tyrant has disposed of foreign enemies by
conquest or treaty, and there is nothing more to fear
from them, then he is always stirring up some war or
other, in order that the people may require a leader.

We are twice armed if we fight with faith.

A VERY UNLUCKY COW

THE BATTLE OF MESSINES (or Mesen, in modern-day Belgium) was a long time in the planning and even longer in the digging. The Allied forces, under the command of Herbert Plumer, had prepared twenty-two mineshafts and five miles of tunnels to hold 600 tonnes of explosives. From 02.50 on the morning of 7 June 1917, an eerie twenty-minute silence followed the end of the preceding week-long artillery bombardment of the German trenches. At 03.10, the simultaneous detonation of the mines lit up the skies of Europe and was reputedly heard by Lloyd George in his study in Downing Street. The explosions took out 10,000 enemy soldiers at a stroke and ensured victory for the Allied forces within hours. Unbelievably, it was the first time on the Western Front that defensive casualties had been higher than those of the attacking side, so up until that point defence had been the best form of attack!

Two of the massive twenty-one mines laid were not detonated and the British lost the details of their precise locations after the war. Lightning found one of the mines in 1955 but casualties were lighter this time – one dead cow. The Belgians think they know where the other one is, although no attempts have been made to recover it. Messines or Benidorm this year, do you think?

HERBERT PLUMER

(1857–1932, BRITISH ARMY COMMANDER)

Gentlemen, we may not make history tomorrow,
but we shall certainly change the geography.

Said to his staff on the eve of the Battle of Messines in June 1917

PLUTARCH

(C. AD 46–120, GRECO-ROMAN HISTORIAN)

There is nothing a Roman enjoys more than the
sight of his commanding officer eating the same
bread as him, or lying on a plain straw mattress, or
lending a hand to dig a ditch or raise a palisade.

MARCO POLO

(C. 1254–1324, VENETIAN MERCHANT AND EXPLORER)

If you put together all the Christians in the
world, with their Emperors and their Kings,
the whole of these Christians – aye, and throw
in the Saracens to boot – would not have such
power, or be able to do so much as this Kublai,
who is Lord of all the Tartars in the world.

Referring to Kublai Khan

They are of all men in the world the best able to
endure exertion and hardship and the least costly
to maintain and therefore the best adapted for
conquering territory and overthrowing kingdoms.

Referring to the Mongol warriors of Kublai Khan

JOHN POPE

(1822–1892, AMERICAN ARMY OFFICER)

Success and glory are in the advance.
Disaster and shame lurk in the rear.

Message to the Army of Virginia, 1862

KING PORUS

(DIED 317 BC, INDIAN RULER)

Treat me like a king.

*His reply when asked by Alexander the Great upon his capture
how he wished to be treated. Alexander was so impressed
that he released Porus and gave him back his kingdom.*

HERBERT V. PROCHNOW

(1897–1998, AMERICAN WRITER AND TOASTMASTER)

A visitor from Mars could easily pick out the civilised
nations. They have the best implements of war.

'CHESTY' PULLER

(1898–1971, UNITED STATES MARINE CORPS COMMANDER)

We're surrounded. That simplifies the problem
of getting to these people and killing them.

Battle of Chosin Reservoir, Korea, 1950

ERNIE PYLE

(1900–1945, AMERICAN WAR CORRESPONDENT)

At last we are in it up to our necks, and everything
is changed, even your outlook on life.
On the entry of America into World War Two.

War makes strange giant creatures out of us
little routine men who inhabit the earth.

The front-line soldier wants it to be got over by
the physical process of his destroying enough
Germans to end it. He is truly at war. The rest
of us, no matter how hard we work, are not.

But to the fighting soldier that phase of the war is
behind. It was left behind after his first battle. His
blood is up. He is fighting for his life, and killing now
for him is as much a profession as writing is for me.
Writing about the initial fear of the unknown

Swinging first and swinging to kill
is all that matters now.

It was a night when London was
ringed and stabbed with fire.
Writing in London during the Blitz

I've been immersed in it too long. My
spirit is wobbly and my mind is confused.
The hurt has become too great.

Their life consisted wholly and solely of war,
for they were and always had been front-line
infantrymen. They survived because the fates
were kind to them, certainly – but also because
they had become hard and immensely wise
in animal-like ways of self-preservation.

Someday when peace has returned to this
odd world I want to come to London again
and stand on a certain balcony on a moonlit
night and look down upon the peaceful silver
curve of the Thames with its dark bridges.

PYRRHUS

(C. 319–272 BC, KING OF EPIRUS AND MACEDON)

Another such victory over the
Romans, and we are undone.

After heavy losses at Asculum, 279 BC

Q

Francis Quarles

(1592–1644, English poet)

Our God and soldiers we alike adore,
Ev'n at the brink of danger; not before:
After deliverance, both alike requited;
Our God's forgotten, and our soldiers slighted.

Let the fear of danger be a spur to prevent it; he
that fears not, gives advantage to the danger.

Salvatore Quasimodo

(1901–1968, Italian writer)

War, I have always said, forces men to
change their standards, regardless of
whether their country has won or lost.

DAN QUAYLE

(BORN 1947, VICE PRESIDENT OF THE UNITED STATES)

We have a firm commitment to NATO [the North Atlantic Treaty Organisation]; we are a part of NATO. We have a firm commitment to Europe. We are a part of Europe.

RAYMOND QUENEAU

(1903–1976, FRENCH WRITER)

There have been only rare moments in history where individual histories were able to run their course without wars or revolutions.

LUDWIG QUIDDE

(1858–1941, GERMAN PACIFIST)

Lightly armed nations can move toward war just as easily as those that are armed to the teeth, and they will do so if the usual causes of war are not removed.

R

WALTER RALEIGH

(C. 1554–1618, BRITISH SOLDIER, EXPLORER AND WRITER)

War begets quiet, quiet idleness, idleness
disorder, disorder ruin; likewise ruin order,
order virtue, virtue glory, and good fortune.

The bodies of men, munition, and money
may justly be called the sinews of war.

Better it were not to live than to live a coward.

WALTER ALEXANDER RALEIGH

(1861–1922, ENGLISH WRITER AND HISTORIAN)

The cavalry, in particular, was not
friendly to the aeroplane, which, it was
believed, would frighten the horses.

JEANNETTE RANKIN

(1880–1973, FIRST AMERICAN CONGRESSWOMAN)

You can no more win a war than
you can win an earthquake.

There can be no compromise with war; it cannot
be reformed or controlled; cannot be disciplined
into decency or codified into common sense.

RONALD REAGAN

(1911–2004, FORTIETH PRESIDENT OF THE UNITED STATES)

Heroes may not be braver than anyone else.
They're just braver five minutes longer.

Peace is not absence of conflict; it is the ability
to handle conflict by peaceful means.

People do not make wars; governments do.

History teaches that wars begin when governments
believe the price of aggression is cheap.

Some people live an entire lifetime and wonder
if they have ever made a difference in the world.
The Marines don't have that problem.

A people free to choose will always choose peace.

Democracy is worth dying for, because
it's the most deeply honourable form of
government ever devised by man.

Above all, we must realise that no arsenal,
or no weapon in the arsenals of the world, is
so formidable as the will and moral courage
of free men and women. It is a weapon our
adversaries in today's world do not have.

The Games more than 2,000 years ago started
as a means of bringing peace between the Greek
city-states. And in those days, even if a war was
going on, they called off the war in order to hold
the Games. I wish we were still as civilised.

HOLD THAT WAR!

The Ancient Olympics were held every four years
between 776 BC and AD 394, and, as Ronald
Reagan rightly reminded us, the Paxa Olympica
(Olympic Truce) was invoked to protect against
unwanted military activity during the month
leading up to the Games and while the Games
were taking place. Heralds would be sent out
to all the corners of the Greek Empire to ensure
that athletes, spectators and officials could travel
safely to and from Olympia. This even happened
in 480 BC, at a time when seventy Greek city-
states, led by the Athenians and the Spartans, were
busy repelling the invasion of Xerxes I during the
Greco-Persian War.

The Modern Olympics have been held every four
years between 1896 and 2012, except on three
occasions, in 1916, 1940 and 1944, when war
stopped play. Spot the difference.

Just think how easy his task and mine might be in
these meetings that we held if suddenly there was
a threat to this world from another planet. We'd
find out once and for all that we really are all
human beings here on this earth together.

On the meetings held between him and Mikhail Gorbachev

Freedom is never more than one generation away
from extinction. We didn't pass it to our children in
the bloodstream. It must be fought for, protected,
and handed on for them to do the same.

RED CLOUD

(1822–1909, SIOUX CHIEF)

We were told that they wished merely to pass
through our country... to seek for gold in the far
west... Yet before the ashes of the council are cold,
the Great Father is building his forts among us. His
presence here is an insult and a threat. It is an insult
to the spirits of our ancestors. Are we then to give
up their sacred graves to be allowed for corn?

CARDINAL RICHELIEU

(1585–1642, FRENCH STATESMAN)

War is one of the scourges with which
it has pleased God to afflict men.

MANFRED VON RICHTHOFEN

(THE RED BARON) (1892–1918, GERMAN ACE FIGHTER PILOT)

With a bullet through his head, he fell from an
altitude of 9,000 feet – a beautiful death.

*In a letter telling of the death of Count
von Holck over Verdun in 1916*

Fight on and fly on to the last drop of blood and
the last drop of fuel, to the last beat of the heart.

It is a pity that my collection of trophies
contains not a single Russian.

The duty of the fighter pilot is to patrol his
area of the sky, and shoot down any enemy
fighters in that area. Anything else is rubbish.

*Von Richthofen would not let pilots under his
command strafe troops in the trenches*

Everything depends on whether we have for
opponents those French tricksters or those daring
rascals, the English. I prefer the English. Frequently
their daring can only be described as stupidity.
In their eyes it may be pluck and daring.

One can become enthusiastic over anything.
For a time I was delighted with bomb
throwing. It gave me a tremendous pleasure
to bomb those fellows from above.

If I should come out of this war alive, I
will have more luck than brains.

In a letter to his mother upon being decorated with the Iron Cross

MERRY CHRISTMAS, RED BARON

LIKE MANY CAVALRY OFFICERS who found that their horses weren't much use in the trenches, Manfred von Richthofen volunteered for the air force. After a spell as an observer/gunner in two-seater aircraft, Manfred decided that the new single-seater front-loaded Fokkers would be much easier to shoot from so he underwent the necessary training, passed all three exams and received his pilot's licence on Christmas Day, 1915.

It would be nine months before his first recognised combat kill, but he would go on to amass a total of eighty enemy hits. In order to commemorate that first kill, he ordered a silver trophy from Berlin with the inscription '1 Vickers 2 17.9.16', which signified: hit number 1; type of aircraft shot down; two enemy fighters on board; and date of hit. He got sixty such trophies on his sideboard before the jeweller ran out of silver, but he had long since found a better way of showing off anyway – by painting his plane bright red. He couldn't have made himself a more glaring target, but it wouldn't be until April 1918 that he was finally taken down. The Allied soldiers on the ground where he crashed stripped his plane bare for souvenirs of the most iconic fighter pilot of the war.

It is better that one's customers come to one's shop than to have to look for them abroad.

Von Richthofen thought this because planes taken down over enemy lines did not count as hits, because they could not be verified on the ground

Of course no one thought of anything except of attacking the enemy. It lies in the instinct of every German to rush at the enemy wherever he meets him, particularly if he meets hostile cavalry.

I started shooting when I was much too far away. That was merely a trick of mine. I did not mean so much as to hit him as to frighten him, and I succeeded in catching him. He began flying curves and this enabled me to draw near.

The English had hit upon a splendid joke. They intended to catch me or to bring me down.

PAUL RODRIGUEZ

(BORN 1955, MEXICAN-AMERICAN COMEDIAN)

I think war might be God's way of teaching us geography.

WILL ROGERS

(1879–1935, AMERICAN COWBOY, ACTOR AND HUMORIST)

You can't say civilisation don't advance… in every war they kill you in a new way.

Diplomats are just as essential in starting a war as soldiers are in finishing it.

ERWIN ROMMEL

(THE DESERT FOX) (1891–1944, GERMAN MILITARY COMMANDER)

In a man-to-man fight, the winner is he who
has one more round in his magazine.

One must not judge everyone in the world
by his qualities as a soldier: otherwise
we should have no civilisation.

Mortal danger is an effective antidote for fixed ideas.

So long as one isn't carrying one's head
under one's arm, things aren't too bad.

Be an example to your men, in your duty and
in private life. Avoid excessive sharpness or
harshness of voice, which usually indicates the
man who has shortcomings of his own to hide.

Courage which goes against military
expediency is stupidity, or, if it is insisted
upon by a commander, irresponsibility.

Don't fight a battle if you don't
gain anything by winning.

In the absence of orders, go find something and kill it.

ELEANOR ROOSEVELT

(1884–1962, FIRST LADY OF THE UNITED STATES)

For it isn't enough to talk about peace,
one must believe in it. And it isn't enough
to believe in it. One must work at it.

I cannot believe that war is the best solution. No one
won the last war, and no one will win the next war.

Hate and force cannot be in just a part of the
world without having an effect on the rest of it.

When will our consciences grow so tender that we will
act to prevent human misery rather than avenge it?

FRANKLIN D. ROOSEVELT

(1882–1945, THIRTY-SECOND PRESIDENT OF THE UNITED STATES)

Hitler built a fortress around Europe,
but he forgot to put a roof on it.

*Speaking about the Allied bombing campaign
over Germany in World War Two, 1942*

Hostilities exist. There is no blinking at the fact that
our people, our territory, and our interests are in
grave danger. With confidence in our armed forces,
with the unbounding determination of our people, we
will gain the inevitable triumph – so help us God.

*Speech to Congress, following the attack on
Pearl Harbour in December 1941*

More than an end to war, we want an end to the beginning of all wars – yes, an end to this brutal, inhuman and thoroughly impractical method of settling the differences between governments.

THEODORE ROOSEVELT

(1858–1919, TWENTY-SIXTH PRESIDENT OF THE UNITED STATES)

If there is not the war, you don't get the great general; if there is not a great occasion, you don't get a great statesman; if Lincoln had lived in a time of peace, no one would have known his name.

JEAN-JACQUES ROUSSEAU

(1712–1778, FRENCH PHILOSOPHER AND WRITER)

War then, is a relation, not between man and man: but between state and state; and individuals are enemies only accidentally: not as men, nor even as citizens: but as soldiers; not as members of their country, but as its defenders.

SALMAN RUSHDIE

(BORN 1947, BRITISH-INDIAN WRITER)

After a long, hopeless war, people will settle for peace, at almost any price.

BERTRAND RUSSELL

(1872–1970, BRITISH PHILOSOPHER)

War does not determine who is right – only who is left.

Why is propaganda so much more successful
when it stirs up hatred than when it
tries to stir up friendly feeling?

During the war they [women] gave a large-
scale refutation of this charge.

On the common opinion that women would tend to be pacifists

You may envy Napoleon, but Napoleon envied
Caesar, Caesar envied Alexander, and Alexander,
I dare say, envied Hercules, who never existed.

Patriots always talk of dying for their country
and never of killing for their country.

WILLIAM HOWARD RUSSELL

(1821–1907, IRISH WAR CORRESPONDENT)

They dashed on towards that thin red
streak tipped with a line of steel.

*Reporting on the Russian charge towards the 93rd Sutherland
Highland Regiment at the Battle of Balaclava in 1854.
Since popularised into 'the thin red line' that describes a
thinly spread military force holding back the enemy.*

ANATOLY RYBAKOV

(1911–1998, SOVIET WRITER)

Death solves all problems – no man, no problem.

S

Antoine de Saint-Exupéry

(1900–1944, French writer and aviation pioneer)

A chief is a man who assumes responsibility. He says,
'I was beaten.' He does not say, 'My men were beaten.'

War is not an adventure. It is a disease. It is like typhus.

Saladin

(1138–1193, sultan of Egypt and Syria)

When I am buried, carry my winding-sheet
on the point of a spear, and say these words:
Behold the spoils, which Saladin carries
with him! Of all his victories, realms, and
riches, nothing remains to him but this.

Reportedly his dying words

SALADIN 1 LIONHEART 1

BY THE TIME SALADIN took Jerusalem in 1187, he had already enjoyed military success in Egypt, Syria, Mesopotamia and Palestine, but it was the taking of Jerusalem that was to raise the hackles of Richard the Lionheart, to the extent that he immediately set off on the Third Crusade. Richard was an accomplished warrior himself, but he soon found himself pitted against a well-educated, chivalrous commander who had secured his victories through a mixture of skilful diplomacy, clever tactics – including the purchase of superior arms from European merchants to use against European armies – and decisive action.

Saladin did not allow his soldiers to kill civilians or inflict unnecessary damage upon the capture of a city, but Richard still ordered the massacre of around 3,000 Saracen soldiers captured at the Battle of Acre. Still Saladin refused to lower himself to the standards of the West. When Richard lost his horse in battle, Saladin sent him two fresh ones; when Richard was wounded, he was offered Saladin's personal physician; when Richard had a fever, Saladin sent him the choicest fruits available to aid his recovery. The war proved inconclusive and in the end the two great leaders settled for a score draw and a peace treaty that allowed Christians to enter Jerusalem unhindered, but probably slightly ashamed, as pilgrims.

The Franks have none of the better
qualities of men, except courage.

Speaking after he defeated the Franks at the Battle of Hattin in 1187

European merchants supply the best weaponry,
thereby contributing to their own defeat.
In a letter to the Caliph of Baghdad

GEORGE SANTAYANA

(1863–1952, SPANISH-AMERICAN PHILOSOPHER)

To delight in war is a merit in the soldier,
a dangerous quality in the captain, and
a positive crime in the statesman.

Wealth, religion and military victory have
more rhetorical than efficacious worth.

Those who cannot remember the past
are condemned to repeat it.

JEAN-PAUL SARTRE

(1905–1980, FRENCH WRITER AND PHILOSOPHER)

When the rich wage war, it's the poor who die.

A lost battle is a battle one thinks one has lost.

Fascism is not defined by the number of its
victims, but by the way it kills them.

If a victory is told in detail, one can no
longer distinguish it from a defeat.

SIEGFRIED SASSOON

(1886–1967, ENGLISH SOLDIER AND POET)

There's things in war one dare not tell
Poor father sitting safe at home, who reads
Of dying heroes and their deathless deeds.

From 'Remorse'

Soldiers are citizens of death's grey land,
Drawing no dividend from time's tomorrows.

From 'Dreamers'

Soldiers are dreamers; when the guns begin
They think of firelit homes, clean beds, and wives.

From 'Dreamers'

I am not protesting against the conduct of the war,
but against the political errors and insincerities
for which the fighting men are being sacrificed.

MAURICE DE SAXE

(1696–1750, GERMAN MARSHAL GENERAL OF FRANCE)

I like people who eat well before
they fight. It is a good sign.

NORMAN SCHWARZKOPF JR

(BORN 1934, AMERICAN ARMY GENERAL)

Leadership is a combination of strategy and character.
If you must be without one, be without the strategy.

Going to war without France is like going
deer hunting without your accordion.

JOHN SEDGWICK

(1813–1864, AMERICAN CIVIL WAR UNION ARMY GENERAL)

They couldn't hit an elephant at this distance.
His last words, just before being killed by a
Confederate bullet on 9 May 1864

COUNT VON SEDGEWICK

(NINETEENTH CENTURY, PRUSSIAN GENERAL)

Let all brave Prussians follow me!
His last words, just prior to being killed by a cannonball

CAROLINE SEEBOHM

(TWENTY-FIRST CENTURY, AMERICAN WRITER)

World War One, that tiresome European engagement
that threatened to close down French couture.

SENECA THE YOUNGER

(C. 4 BC–AD 65, ROMAN PHILOSOPHER AND STATESMAN)

Constant exposure to dangers will
breed contempt for them.

MICHAEL SERVETUS

(1511–1553, SPANISH THEOLOGIAN)

To kill a man is not to defend a
doctrine, but to kill a man.

HENRY SEYMOUR

(SIXTEENTH CENTURY, BRITISH NAVAL COMMANDER)

You have fought more with your pen than many have
in our English Navy fought with their enemies.

*Writing to Francis Walsingham, spymaster to Elizabeth
I, to commend him on his intelligence gathering*

SHAKA

(C. 1787–1828, ZULU LEADER)

Up! Children of Zulu, your day has
come. Up! And destroy them all!

Strike an enemy once and for all. Let him cease to exist
as a tribe or he will live to fly in your throat again.

I need no bodyguard at all, for even the bravest
men who approach me get weak at the knees
and their hearts turn to water, whilst their
heads become giddy and incapable of thinking
as the sweat of fear paralyses them.

WILLIAM SHAKESPEARE
(1564–1616, ENGLISH PLAYWRIGHT)

Cry 'Havoc!' and let slip the dogs of war.
Julius Caesar

Cowards die many times before their deaths;
The valiant never taste death but once.
Julius Caesar

The fire-eyed maid of smoky war
All hot and bleeding will we offer them.
Henry IV, Part I

That I may truly say with the hook-
nosed fellow of Rome,
I came, I saw, and overcame.
Henry IV, Part II

There are few die well that die in a battle.
Henry V

Once more unto the breach, dear friends, once more;
Or close the wall up with our English dead.
In peace there's nothing so becomes a man
As modest stillness and humility:
But when the blast of war blows in our ears,
Then imitate the action of the tiger;
Stiffen the sinews, summon up the blood…
Follow your spirit, and upon this charge
Cry 'God for Harry, England, and Saint George!'
*Henry V, as the king urged his troops to attack once
more through the breach in the city wall of Harfleur*

From now until the end of the world,
we and it shall be remembered.
We few, we happy few, we band of brothers.
For he today that sheds his blood with me
Shall be my brother.

*Henry V, part of the king's motivational speech
before the Battle of Agincourt*

TWO FINGERS TO THE FRENCH?

AGINCOURT SAW ONE OF the most surprising results
in military history, as the 4,000 longbow archers
of Henry V defeated a 25,000-strong army of
French knights and pikemen backed by Genovese
mercenaries equipped with state-of-the-art Italian
crossbows. According to some English historians,
the French lost as many as 10,000 men against
English losses of only 100–300. A number of
factors contributed to this lopsided outcome:
superior English tactics, the heavy rain that caused
the heavily armoured French knights to sink in the
mud up to their hips, the presence of the English
king on the battlefield (the French king, Charles
VI, was a sickly chap and couldn't make it), and
the speed with which the skilful English archers
could reload.

It has been said that the French were so enraged
that they threatened henceforth to amputate
the two fingers that held the bowstring of any
captured English archers, and that the English
archers responded by waving their index and
middle fingers at the French from the top of their
ramparts, the two-finger salute that even today is
one of the highest insults that can be inflicted by
body language alone.

Sound trumpets! let our bloody colours wave!
And either victory, or else a grave.
Henry VI, Part III

Let me have war, say I,
It exceeds peace as far as day does night,
It's spritely waking, audible, and full of vent.
Coriolanus

Had I a dozen sons, each in my love alike... I
had rather eleven die nobly for their country
than one voluptuously surfeit out of action.
Coriolanus

I will not yield,
To kiss the ground before young Malcolm's feet,
And to be baited with the rabble's curse.
Though Birnam wood be come to Dunsinane,
And thou opposed, being of no woman born,
Yet I will try the last. Before my body
I throw my warlike shield. Lay on, Macduff,
And damn'd be him that first cries, 'Hold, enough!'
*Macbeth in Macbeth, spoken before his
decisive (losing) battle with Macduff*

He is come to open
The purple testament of bleeding war.
Richard II

Fight, gentlemen of England! Fight, bold yeomen!
Draw, archers, draw your arrows to the head!
Spur your proud horses hard, and ride in blood;
Amaze the welkin with your broken staves!
Richard III

And all the gods go with you! Upon your sword
Sit laurel victory! And smooth success
Be strewed before your feet!

Anthony and Cleopatra

THE FEMALE OF THE SPECIES...

ROZA SHANINA WAS A Red Army sniper during
World War Two. She was twenty years of age
when she arrived on the front line on 2 April 1944
and in no time at all it became clear that she was
going to be more effective even than many of the
battle-hardened male veterans. In a six-day period
starting on 6 April, she killed thirteen German
soldiers while under artillery and machine-gun
fire. When around fifty enemy soldiers attacked
the trench she shared with some other female
snipers, it is reported that the girls took out a
number of them with well-aimed bullets before
finishing some of the others off with bayonets,
grenades and the shovels they had used to dig
their trench in the first place. Roza was shot in the
shoulder in December 1944 but was back in action
within days. The following month she was fatally
wounded in the chest while shielding the badly
wounded commander of an artillery unit.

In addition to her sniper log, Roza Shanina also
kept a combat diary, in which, in order to preserve
military secrecy, she referred to the killed as
'blacks' and the wounded as 'reds'. Roza herself
was credited with a grand total of fifty-four
'blacks'.

ROZA GEORGIYEVNA SHANINA

(1924–1945, SOVIET SOLDIER)

I have done no more than is my duty as a Soviet citizen, having stood up to defend the motherland.

If it turns necessary to die for the common happiness, then I'm ready to.
Two excerpts from her combat diary

GEORGE BERNARD SHAW

(1856–1950, IRISH PLAYWRIGHT)

When the military man approaches, the world locks up its spoons and packs off its womankind.

Patriotism is your conviction that this country is superior to all others because you were born in it.

[An Englishman] does everything on principle.
He fights you on patriotic principles;
he robs you on business principles; he
enslaves you on imperial principles.

PERCY BYSSHE SHELLEY

(1792–1822, ENGLISH POET)

War is the statesman's game, the priest's delight, the lawyer's jest, the hired assassin's trade.

RICHARD BRINSLEY SHERIDAN

(1751–1816, ANGLO-IRISH PLAYWRIGHT AND POLITICIAN)

There's only one truth about war: people die.

WILLIAM TECUMSEH SHERMAN

(1820–1891, AMERICAN CIVIL WAR UNION ARMY GENERAL)

The scenes on this field would have
cured anybody of war.

After the Battle of Shiloh in 1862

Grant stood by me when I was crazy, and
I stood by him when he was drunk, and
now we stand by each other always.

*Referring to the mutual respect that existed
between himself and Ulysses S. Grant*

I intend to make Georgia howl.

*The promise he made to Ulysses S. Grant before
marching his army south to take Savannah in 1864*

I beg to present you as a Christmas
gift the city of Savannah.

*In a telegraph to Abraham Lincoln, after capturing
Savannah on 21 December 1864*

I think I understand what military fame is;
to be killed on the field of battle and have
your name misspelled in the newspapers.

War is cruelty. There's no use trying to reform
it; the crueller it is, the sooner it'll be over.

If I had my choice I would kill every reporter
in the world, but I am sure we would be
getting reports from Hell before breakfast.

SHIBA YOSHIMASA

(1350–1410, JAPANESE LORD AND WARRIOR)

The man whose profession is arms should calm
his mind and look into the depths of others'.
Doing so is likely the best of the martial arts.

Generally speaking, when combat is bound to be
easy, you let the other side make the first move. When
it's going to be dangerous, you should consider it
your task alone, even if it takes a hundred tries.

LOUIS SIMPSON

(BORN 1923, AMERICAN POET)

Being shelled… means lying face down and contracting
your body into as small a space as possible.

The aim of military training is not just to prepare
men for battle, but to make them long for it.

GOBIND SINGH

(1666–1708, TENTH OF THE ELEVEN SIKH GURUS)

Sword that smites in a flash,
That scatters the armies of the wicked
In the great battle-field,
O symbol of the brave.
Your arm is irresistible, your brightness shines forth
The splendour of the black dazzles like the sun.
Sword, you are the scourge of saints,
You are the scourge of the wicked;
Scatterer of sinners, I take refuge with you.
Hail to the Creator. Saviour and sustainer,
Hail to you: Sword supreme!

*Explaining why the sword (or Kirpan) can
be used against the forces of evil*

SITTING BULL

(1831–1890, SIOUX CHIEF)

I am a red man. If the Great Spirit had desired me
to be a white man he would have made me so in
the first place. He put in your heart certain wishes
and plans, in my heart he put other and different
desires. Each man is good in his sight. It is not
necessary for Eagles to be Crows. We are poor... but
we are free. No white man controls our footsteps.
If we must die... we die defending our rights.

I wish it to be remembered that I was the last
man of my tribe to surrender my rifle.

Is it wrong for me to love my own? Is it wicked for
me because my skin is red? Because I am Sioux?
Because I was born where my father lived? Because
I would die for my people and my country?

WILLIAM SLIM

(1891–1970, BRITISH MILITARY COMMANDER)

The first duty of an advance guard is to advance.

Morale, only morale, individual morale
as a foundation under training and
discipline, will bring victory.

*Address to the officers of the 10th Indian
Infantry Division in June 1941*

Now, gentlemen, we are kicking our
Japanese neighbours back to Rangoon.

After the enforced retreat from Burma in 1942

These are the things that make men go on
fighting even though terror grips their heart.

On a soldier's senses of duty and shame

OLIVER P. SMITH

(1893–1977, UNITED STATES MARINE CORPS GENERAL)

Retreat, hell! We're just attacking
in a different direction.

SOCRATES

(C. 469–399 BC, GREEK PHILOSOPHER)

A disorderly mob is no more an army than
a heap of building materials is a house.

SOLON

(C. 638–558 BC, GREEK MORALIST AND LAWMAKER)

Learn to obey before you command.

SOPHOCLES

(C. 497–405 BC, GREEK TRAGEDIAN)

It is the brave man's part to live
with glory, or with glory die.

SPOTTED TAIL

(1823–1881, SIOUX CHIEF)

This war did not spring up on our land, this war was
brought upon us by the children of the Great Father
who came to take our land without a price, and who,
in our land, do a great many evil things… This war has
come from robbery – from the stealing of our land.

JOSEPH STALIN

(1878–1953, SOVIET DICTATOR)

[We] must fight for every inch of Soviet soil, fight
to the last drop of blood... onward, to victory!

Everyone imposes his own system
as far as his army can reach.

Ideas are more powerful than guns. We
would not let our enemies have guns,
why should we let them have ideas?

In the Soviet army it takes more
courage to retreat than advance.

The only real power comes out of a long rifle.

You cannot make a revolution with silk gloves.

ROBERT LOUIS STEVENSON

(1850–1894, SCOTTISH WRITER)

This is the officer's part to make men continue
to do things, they know not wherefore, and
when, if choice was offered, they would lie
down where they were and be killed.

Kidnapped

JACK STRAW

(BORN 1946, BRITISH POLITICIAN)

Our eventual aim is simply stated – that there should be no safe haven for terrorists anywhere in the world.

Speaking after the attacks on the twin towers of the World Trade Centre in September 2001

SUBUTAI

(1176–1248, MONGOLIAN MILITARY STRATEGIST)

Honour is nothing without victory.

CHARLES SUMNER

(1811–1874, AMERICAN POLITICIAN)

Give me the money that has been spent in war and I will clothe every man, woman, and child in an attire of which kings and queens will be proud. I will build a schoolhouse in every valley over the whole earth.

SUN TZU

(C. 544–496 BC, CHINESE MILITARY STRATEGIST AND GENERAL)

All warfare is based on deception.

Know the enemy and know yourself; in a hundred battles you will never be in peril.

Let your plans be dark and as impenetrable as
night, and when you move, fall like a thunderbolt.

He who knows when he can fight and
when he cannot will be victorious.

Victory is reserved for those who
are willing to pay its price.

Management of many is the same as management
of few. It is a matter of organisation.

In war, numbers alone confer no advantage. Do
not advance relying on sheer military power.

The general who advances without coveting fame
and retreats without fearing disgrace, whose only
thought is to protect his country and do good service
for his sovereign, is the jewel of the kingdom.

The general who wins the battle makes
many calculations in his temple before
his battle is fought. The general who loses
makes but few calculations beforehand.

The best victory is when the opponent surrenders
of its own accord before there are any actual
hostilities... It is best to win without fighting.

To capture the enemy's entire army is better than to destroy it. For to win one hundred victories in one battle is not the supreme of excellence. To subdue the enemy without fighting is the supreme excellence.

There is no instance of a nation benefitting from prolonged warfare.

ALEXANDER SUVOROV

(1730–1800, RUSSIAN GENERAL)

What is difficult in training will become easy in a battle.

The bullet is a mad thing; only the bayonet knows what it is about.

Perish yourself but rescue your comrade.

One minute can decide the outcome of the battle; one hour, the outcome of the campaign; and one day, the fate of the country.

When the enemy is driven back, we have failed; but when he is cut off, circled and dispersed, we have succeeded.

The Church will pray to God for the dead.
The survivor has honour and glory.

If we had not driven them into hell…
hell would have swallowed us.

PUBLILIUS SYRUS

(FIRST CENTURY BC, SYRIAN WRITER)

It is a bad plan that cannot be altered.

He is best secure from dangers who is on
his guard even when he seems safe.

T

TACITUS

(AD 56–117, ROMAN HISTORIAN AND SENATOR)

Even the bravest are frightened by sudden terrors.

The proper arts of a general are
judgment and prudence.

The desire for safety stands against
every great and noble enterprise.

Valour is the contempt of death and pain.

Great empires are not maintained by timidity.

TECUMSEH
(1768–1813, SHAWNEE CHIEF)

When it comes time to die, be not like those whose hearts are filled with the fear of death, so when their time comes they weep and pray for a little more time to live their lives over again in a different way. Sing your death song, and die like a hero going home.

ALFRED, LORD TENNYSON
(1809–1892, ENGLISH POET)

Half a league, half a league,
Half a league onward,
All in the valley of Death
Rode the six hundred:
'Forward, the Light Brigade!
Charge for the guns' he said:
Into the valley of Death
Rode the six hundred.
'Forward, the Light Brigade!'
Was there a man dismay'd?
Not tho' the soldier knew
Someone had blunder'd:
Theirs not to make reply,
Theirs not to reason why,
Theirs but to do and die:
Into the valley of Death
Rode the six hundred.

From 'The Charge of the Light Brigade'

ECATERINA TEODOROIU

(1894–1917, ROMANIAN SOLDIER)

Forward, men, I'm still with you!

Her reported last words after being hit by German machine-gun fire

---

A ROMANIAN JOAN OF ARC

WHEN ROMANIA ENTERED WORLD War One in 1916, the twenty-two-year-old Ecaterina was a schoolteacher. She immediately enlisted as a field nurse. Impressed by the courage of the wounded she tended to, and spurred on by the death of her soldier brother, she eventually convinced reluctant Romanian commanders that she should be sent into combat on the front line. Having been taken prisoner, she escaped by killing at least two German soldiers. She was then wounded and hospitalised, but soon came back to the front where she proved herself so capable that she was promoted to Second Lieutenant and given command of a twenty-five-strong platoon.

She was killed in September 1917 when she was hit by enemy machine-gun fire. 'Forward, men, I'm still with you' were her reported last words. It was so unusual for a woman at that time to fight in the thick of battle, let alone command and gain the respect of the men around her, that Ecaterina Teodoroiu is still revered in Romania today with Joan-of-Arc proportions. Some Romanians have probably watched the films made of her heroic exploits as often as some of us have watched *The Bridge on the River Kwai*.

TERENCE

(C. 190–159 BC, ROMAN PLAYWRIGHT)

Fortes fortuna adiuvat.
(Fortune favours the brave.)

JOHN TERRAINE

(1921–2003, BRITISH MILITARY HISTORIAN)

[They] had become what they were to remain for the rest of the war – the spearhead of the British Army.

Commenting on the fighting capability of the Australian and New Zealand troops in World War One

A casualty is a man blown to pieces, disintegrated, nothing left of him but a name on a war memorial.

MARGARET THATCHER

(BORN 1925, BRITISH PRIME MINISTER)

Failure? The possibilities do not exist.

Paraphrasing Queen Victoria, on the proposed military action in the Falklands in 1982

Being powerful is like being a lady. If you have to tell people you are, you aren't.

We knew what we had to do and we went about
it and did it. Great Britain is great again.

Referring to the Falklands War

It has been said that... British patriotism
was rediscovered in those spring
days. It was never really lost.

Referring to the Falklands War

Being powerful is like being a lady. If you
have to tell people you are, you aren't.

I don't want to fight any wars; if you can get them
off before we get there, you do it, but off they go.

*To US Secretary of State, Alexander Haig, referring to the
Argentine forces that had invaded the Falklands, while
British ships were on their way to the South Atlantic*

Democratic nations must try to find ways to
starve the terrorist and the hijacker of the
oxygen of publicity on which they depend.

JULIAN THOMPSON

(BORN 1934, ROYAL MARINES COMMANDER
AND MILITARY HISTORIAN)

Be pleased to inform Her Majesty that
the White Ensign flies alongside the
Union Jack... God Save the Queen.

*Cable to London reporting the recapture of South
Georgia from the Argentinians in 1982*

JAMES THOMSON

(1700–1748, SCOTTISH POET AND PLAYWRIGHT)

When Britain first, at Heaven's command
Arose from out the azure main;
This was the charter of the land,
And guardian angels sang this strain:
'Rule, Britannia! Rule the waves:
Britons never will be slaves.'

*From 'Rule Brittania', written by Thomson and
set to music by Thomas Arne in 1740*

HENRY DAVID THOREAU

(1817–1862, AMERICAN WRITER AND PHILOSOPHER)

What is human warfare but just this; an effort to make
the laws of God and nature take sides with one party.

Thank God, men cannot as yet fly, and lay
waste the sky as well as the earth.

THUCYDIDES

(C. 460–395 BC, GREEK HISTORIAN)

A collision at sea can ruin your entire day.

War is not so much a matter of weapons as of money.

Self-control is the chief element in self-respect,
and self-respect is the chief element in courage.

The strong do what they can, and the
weak suffer what they must.

Wars spring from unseen and generally
insignificant causes, the first outbreak
being often but an explosion of anger.

The bravest are surely those who have the clearest
vision of what is before them, glory and danger
alike, and yet notwithstanding, go out to meet it.

Be convinced that to be happy means to be
free and that to be free means to be brave.
Therefore do not take lightly the perils of war.

Time magazine

(12 June 1939)

The French army is still the strongest all-
around fighting machine in Europe.

Tōgō Heihachirō

(1848–1934, Japanese Imperial Navy
commander and fleet admiral)

If your sword is too short, take one step forward.

TOKUGAWA IEYASU

(1543–1616, JAPANESE SHOGUN)

To come to know your enemy, first you must become his friend, and once you become his friend, all his defences come down. Then you can choose the most fitting method for his demise.

J. R. R. TOLKIEN

(1892–1973, ENGLISH WRITER)

I do not love the bright sword for its sharpness, nor the arrow for its swiftness... [but for] that which they defend.

The Two Towers

LEO TOLSTOY

(1828–1910, RUSSIAN WRITER)

In all history there is no war that was not hatched by the governments, the governments alone, independent of the interests of the people, to whom war is always pernicious even when successful.

War on the other hand is such a terrible thing, that no man, especially a Christian man, has the right to assume the responsibility of starting it.

War is so unjust and ugly that all who wage it must try to stifle the voice of conscience within themselves.

LEON TROTSKY

(1879–1940, RUSSIAN MARXIST REVOLUTIONARY)

There are no absolute rules of conduct, either in peace or war. Everything depends on circumstances.

Where force is necessary, there it must be applied boldly, decisively and completely.

Not believing in force is the same as not believing in gravity.

Ideas that enter the mind under fire remain there securely and forever.

Under all conditions well-organised violence seems to him the shortest distance between two points.

TRƯNG TRẮC

(C. AD 12–43, VIETNAMESE REVOLUTIONARY LEADER)

Foremost, I will avenge my country,
Second, I will restore the Hung lineage,
Third, I will avenge the death of my husband,
Lastly, I vow that these goals will be accomplished.

*Following the death of her husband at the hands
of a Chinese commander in* AD 40

SISTERS WERE DOING IT
FOR THEMSELVES

TRƯNG TRẮC AND HER sister, Trưng Nhị, are national heroines in Vietnam. For three years, from AD 40 onwards, they led the first serious resistance movement against the occupying Chinese for 247 years. They had been born into a military family and had grown up learning the martial arts and being very aware of the cruelties of the occupying force. When Trưng Trắc's husband, a would-be rebel leader himself, was executed as an example to others, the sisters decided that enough was enough.

They assembled a large army consisting mostly of women. Legend has it that, to gain the confidence of the people, they killed a man-eating tiger and wrote a proclamation on its skin to urge the people to follow them. Within months, they had taken back sixty-five citadels from the Chinese. They became queens of the country and managed to resist subsequent Chinese attacks for over two years. When they were finally overcome, they chose suicide, the traditional Vietnamese way of maintaining honour, by drowning themselves in a river.

Today they are immortalised in the names of temples, schools and streets, as well as an entire district in Hanoi. An annual holiday is held in their honour. They are commemorated in stories, poems, plays, postage stamps, posters and monuments. In other words, if you're Vietnamese, you know who the Trưng sisters were.

HARRIET TUBMAN

(1820–1913, AMERICAN CIVIL WAR UNION ARMY SPY)

We saw the lightning and that was the gun and then we heard the thunder and that was the big guns; and then we heard the rain falling and that was the blood falling; and when we came to get in the crops, it was dead men that we reaped.

KURT TUCHOLSKY

(1890–1935, GERMAN JOURNALIST AND WRITER)

The war? I can't find it too terrible! The death of one man: that is a catastrophe. One hundred thousand deaths: that is a statistic!

MARK TWAIN

(1835–1910, AMERICAN WRITER)

Courage is resistance to fear, mastery of fear – not absence of fear.

And always we had wars, and more wars, and still other wars all over Europe, all over the world. 'Sometimes in the private interest of royal families,' Satan said, 'sometimes to crush a weak nation; but never a war started by the aggressor for any clean purpose. There is no such war in the history of the race.'

The Mysterious Stranger

History teaches us that whenever a weak and ignorant people possess a thing that a strong and enlightened people want, it must be yielded up peaceably.

Man is the only animal that deals in that atrocity of atrocities, War. He is the only one that gathers his brethren about him and goes forth in cold blood and calm pulse to exterminate his kind. And in the intervals between campaigns he washes the blood off his hands and works for 'the universal brotherhood of man' – with his mouth.

NATHAN F. TWINING

(1897–1982, AMERICAN AIR FORCE GENERAL)

A top World War Two ace once said that fighter pilots fall into two broad categories: those who go out to kill and those who, secretly, desperately, know they are going to get killed – the hunters and the hunted.

If our air forces are never used, they have achieved their finest goal.

U

MORIHEI UESHIBA

(1883–1969, JAPANESE MARTIAL ARTIST)

Those who seek to compete and better one
another are making a terrible mistake.

The real Way of a Warrior is... the
Art of Peace, the power of love.

Aiki... is the way to reconcile the world
and make human beings one family.

When facing the realm of life and death in
the form of an enemy's sword, one must
be firmly settled in mind and body.

Umar ibn Al-Khattab

(C. 588–644, Islamic caliph)

Paradise is under the shadow of our swords. Forward!

Leon Uris

(1924–2003, American writer)

A soldier has one item that can't be neglected. His feet. They are his wheels, his mechanised warfare.

Peter Ustinov

(1921–2004, English actor and writer)

Terrorism is the war of the poor, and war is the terrorism of the rich.

V

PAUL VALÉRY

(1871–1945, FRENCH PHILOSOPHER AND POET)

War is a massacre of people who don't know each other for the profit of people who know each other but don't massacre each other.

Two dangers constantly threaten the world: order and disorder.

PUBLIUS FLAVIUS VEGETIUS RENATUS

(VEGETIUS) (FOURTH CENTURY AD, ROMAN WRITER)

Few men are born brave; many become so through training and force of discipline.

A general is not easily overcome who can form a true judgement of his own and the enemy's forces.

What can a warrior do who charges
when out of breath?

Let him who desires peace prepare for war.

An adversary is more hurt by
desertion than by slaughter.

The courage of a soldier is heightened by
the knowledge of his profession.

We die today not only for our friends and family
but for our gods and for our forefathers and men
before them so pray to them to make us victorious.

PAUL VERLAINE

(1844–1896, FRENCH POET)

Les sanglots longs
Des violins
De l'automne
Blessent mon coeur
D'une longueur
Monotone.
(The long sobbing
Of Autumn's
Violins
Wound my heart
With a monotonous
Langour.)

*The first verse of 'Chanson d'Automne' ('Autumn Song'),
one of France's most popular poems. This verse was
broadcast from London in two stages before the D-Day
landings to alert the French Resistance to the fact that
Operation Overlord was about to get underway.*

LONDON CALLING

Radio Londres was set up in June 1940 to allow the Free French Forces to broadcast to their people back home in Nazi-occupied France. It served to counter the Nazi propaganda of Radio Paris and Radio Vichy and to get messages to the French resistance movements.

Each broadcast would start with: 'Before we begin, please listen to some personal messages,' which clearly were coded messages, seemingly without context. 'I bumped into Napoleon last week' might be a coded instruction to a particular resistance group, whereas 'The arrow would appear to be lodged quite deep' might just be a piece of nonsense to give the enemy the false impression that something was about to go down.

The first three lines of Paul Verlaine's poem were broadcast on 1 June 1944 to let the resistance movements know that the D-Day landings were to begin within two weeks. The second three lines were broadcast on 5 June to let them know that they would start within forty-eight hours. In the event, they did of course get underway the following day.

The job of the resistance fighters was then to scupper in any way possible the ability of the Germans to get reinforcements to the Normandy beaches.

QUEEN VICTORIA

(1819–1901, QUEEN OF GREAT BRITAIN AND
IRELAND AND EMPRESS OF INDIA)

We are not interested in the possibilities
of defeat; they do not exist.

Upon the outbreak of the Boer War in South Africa in 1899

VITELLIUS

(AD 15–69, ROMAN EMPEROR)

The corpse of an enemy always smells sweet.

VLAD THE IMPALER

(1431–1476, PRINCE AND RULER OF WALLACHIA)

We killed 23,884 Bulgars without counting those
whom we burned in homes or the Turks whose
heads were cut by our soldiers… Thus, your
highness, you must know that I have broken
the peace with him (Sultan Mehmet II).

*In a letter to the Hungarian king Corvinus, with whom he had
formed an alliance against Sultan Mehmet II of the Ottoman Empire*

It would be better that those who think
of death should not follow me.

*Before leading his army into battle in The
Night Attack of Târgovişte in 1462*

VOLTAIRE

(1694–1778, FRENCH WRITER AND PHILOSOPHER)

It is forbidden to kill; therefore all murderers
are punished unless they kill in large
numbers and to the sound of trumpets.

An admiral has to be put to death now
and then to encourage the others.

Candide

God is not on the side of the big battalions,
but on the side of those who shoot best.

Those who can make you believe absurdities
can make you commit atrocities.

W

KURT WALDHEIM

(1918–2007, AUSTRIAN DIPLOMAT AND UN SECRETARY-GENERAL)

There is no such thing as collective guilt.

WILLIAM WALLACE

(C. 1272–1305, SCOTTISH INDEPENDENCE LEADER)

We come here with no peaceful intent,
but ready for battle, determined to avenge
our wrongs and set our country free.

Addressed to the Scottish troops before the Battle of Stirling Bridge

I can not be a traitor, for I owe him no
allegiance. He is not my Sovereign; he never
received my homage; and whilst life is in this
persecuted body, he never shall receive it.

From his statement at his trial in 1305, referring to King Edward I

A BRIDGE TOO FAR, OR
JUST TOO NARROW?

Sir William Wallace, the Knight of Elderslie, was
one of the main leaders during the Wars of Scottish
Independence. He was reputedly a physical giant
of a man, and well deserving of his 'Braveheart'
status (you didn't square up to the aggression
of Edward I if you weren't hard enough!). His
reputation stemmed more than anything from
the defeat of the English troops at Stirling Bridge
in 1297, despite being vastly outnumbered. The
bridge was narrow and the English were reputedly
foolish enough to cross only three abreast, which
meant the Scots only had to pick a few of them
off at a time! The bridge is said to have eventually
collapsed under the weight of the English, dead
and alive. Many of them survived death on the
bridge only to drown in the waters below.

Wallace did not, however, die as gloriously as he
had lived. He was hanged, drawn and quartered,
his head tarred and spiked on London Bridge,
and his limbs displayed, separately, in Newcastle,
Berwick, Stirling and Perth.

FRANCIS WALSINGHAM

(1532–1590, English spymaster to Elizabeth I)

Intelligence is never too dear.

ARTEMUS WARD

(1834–1867, AMERICAN HUMORIST)

I have already given two cousins to the war and
I stand ready to sacrifice my wife's brother.

GEORGE WASHINGTON

(1732–1799, FIRST PRESIDENT OF THE UNITED STATES)

If we desire to avoid insult, we must be able to
repel it; if we desire to secure peace, one of the most
powerful instruments of our rising prosperity, it must
be known, that we are at all times ready for war.

Let us therefore animate and encourage each
other, and show the whole world that a Freeman
contending for Liberty on his own ground is
superior to any slavish mercenary on earth.

An army formed of good officers
moves like clockwork.

Every post is honourable in which
a man can serve his country.

Discipline is the soul of an army. It makes
small numbers formidable, procures success
to the weak, and esteem to all.

War – an act of violence, whose object is to
restrain the enemy and to accomplish our will.

Experience teaches us that it is much easier to prevent an enemy from posting themselves than it is to dislodge them after they have got possession.

My first wish is to see this plague of mankind, war, banished from the earth.

When we assumed the Soldier, we did not lay aside the Citizen.

JEAN DE WAVRIN

(C. 1398–1474, FRENCH SOLDIER AND CHRONICLER)

When the battalions of the French were thus formed, it was grand to see them; and as far as one could judge by the eye, they were in number fully six times as many as the English.

From his eyewitness account of the Battle of Agincourt, 1415

SIMONE WEIL

(1909–1943, FRENCH PHILOSOPHER AND ACTIVIST)

Petroleum is a more likely cause of international conflict than wheat.

What a country calls its vital interests are not things that help its people live, but things that help it make war.

Who were the fools who spread the story that brute force cannot kill ideas? Nothing is easier. And once they are dead they are no more than corpses.

It is not the cause for which men took up arms that makes a victory more just or less, it is the order that is established when arms have been laid down.

A self-respecting nation is ready for anything, including war, except for a renunciation of its option to make war.

ARTHUR WELLESLEY

(THE DUKE OF WELLINGTON) (1769–1852, BRITISH FIELD MARSHAL AND PRIME MINISTER)

Our army is composed of the scum of the earth – the mere scum of the earth. It is only wonderful that we should be able to make so much out of them afterwards.

When other Generals make mistakes, their armies are beaten; when I get into a hole, my men pull me out of it.

After the Battle of Waterloo, 1815

We have always been, we are, and I hope that we always shall be detested in France.

An extraordinary affair. I gave them their orders and they wanted to stay and discuss them.

It has been a damned nice thing – the nearest run thing you ever saw in your life... By God! I don't think it would have been done if I had not been there.

Speaking about Waterloo

Nothing except a battle lost can be half
as melancholy as a battle won.

The only thing I am afraid of is fear.

I used to say of him that his presence on the field
made the difference of forty thousand men.
Speaking of Napoleon

All the business of war, and indeed all the business
of life, is to endeavour to find out what you
don't know by what you do; that's what I called
'guessing what was at the other side of the hill.'

Hard pounding this, gentlemen. Let's
see who pounds the longest.
At the Battle of Waterloo

H. G. WELLS

(1866–1946, BRITISH WRITER)

If we don't end war, war will end us.

It is not reasonable that those who gamble with
men's lives should not stake their own.

My imagination refuses to see any sort of
submarine doing anything but suffocating
its crew and floundering at sea.

Once the command of the air is obtained…
the war must become a conflict between
a seeing host and one that is blind.

WILLIAM WESTMORELAND

(1914–2005, AMERICAN ARMY GENERAL)

Vietnam was the first war ever fought without
any censorship. Without censorship, things can
get terribly confused in the public mind.

WALT WHITMAN

(1819–1892, AMERICAN POET AND JOURNALIST)

Beautiful that war and all its deeds of
carnage must in time be utterly lost.
From 'Reconciliation'

OSCAR WILDE

(1854–1900, IRISH WRITER AND POET)

Always forgive your enemies – nothing
annoys them so much.

As long as war is regarded as wicked, it will
always have its fascination. When it is looked
upon as vulgar, it will cease to be popular.

A thing is not necessarily true because a man dies for it.

Patriotism is the virtue of the vicious.

241

WILLIAM III

(1650–1702, KING OF ENGLAND, SCOTLAND,
IRELAND AND PRINCE OF ORANGE)

There is one certain means by which I can be sure to never see my country's ruin: I will die in the last ditch.

WOODROW WILSON

(1856–1924, TWENTY-EIGHTH PRESIDENT OF THE UNITED STATES)

In every discussion of peace that must end this war, it is taken for granted that the peace must be followed by some definite concert of power which will make it virtually impossible that any such catastrophe should ever overwhelm us again.

From his address to Congress in January 1917, in which he sought approval to enter the war against Germany

Is there any man, is there any woman, let me say any child here that does not know that the seed of war in the modern world is industrial and commercial rivalry?

The history of liberty is a history of resistance.

JAMES WOLFE

(1727–1759, BRITISH ARMY OFFICER)

What, do they run already? Then I die happy.

His dying words on being told that Quebec had fallen

GREAT LEADERS OF A FEATHER...

JAMES WOLFE JOINED THE army when he was just thirteen and by the time he was twenty-one, he had already served with distinction at home and abroad. He came to the attention of George II and the prime minister, William Pitt (the Elder), during the early stages of the Seven Years' War with France, leading ultimately to his appointment as leader of the assault on Quebec in 1759.

The French under Montcalm were well entrenched on high ground. After three months of British siege yielded almost nothing, Wolfe led 200 ships, 9,000 soldiers and 18,000 sailors to the base of the cliffs along the St Lawrence River – a very perilous move. His army, with two small cannons, scaled the cliffs early the next morning, surprising the French who had assumed that the cliffs were too steep to be climbed. The French were defeated after only fifteen minutes of battle, but Wolfe himself was fatally wounded.

Today his statue shares the town green in Westerham, Kent (where he was born) with that of a certain Winston Churchill, who moved into the neighbourhood a couple of hundred years later. They must have some stories to share in the dead of night, those two.

Possessed with a full confidence of the certain success
which British valour must gain over such enemies, I
have led you up these steep and dangerous rocks, only
solicitous to show you the foe within your reach.

After scaling the cliffs at the Battle of Quebec in 1759

The impossibility of a retreat makes no difference
in the situation of men resolved to conquer
or die; and, believe me, my friends, if your
conquest could be bought with the blood of your
general, he would most cheerfully resign a life
which he has long devoted to his country.

VIRGINIA WOOLF

(1882–1941, ENGLISH WRITER)

If you insist upon fighting to protect me, or 'our'
country, let it be understood soberly and rationally
between us that you are fighting to gratify a sex
instinct that I cannot share; to procure benefits where
I have not shared and probably will not share.

Three Guineas

The connection between dress and war is not far to
seek; your finest clothes are those you wear as soldiers.

We can best help you to prevent war not by repeating
your words and following your methods but by
finding new words and creating new methods.

Three Guineas

ORVILLE WRIGHT

(1871–1948, AVIATION PIONEER)

When my brother and I built the first man-carrying flying machine we thought that we were introducing into the world an invention that would make further wars practically impossible.

I regret all the terrible damage caused by fire, but... it is possible to put fire to thousands of important uses.

Analogy used when asked during World War Two if he ever regretted being involved in the invention of the aeroplane

WU KUNG-TSAO

(1902–1983, CHINESE MARTIAL ARTS TEACHER)

Bravery without forethought causes a man to fight blindly and desperately like a mad bull. Such an opponent must not be encountered with brute force, but may be lured into an ambush and slain.

X

XENOPHON

(C. 430–354 BC, GREEK HISTORIAN, SOLDIER AND PHILOSOPHER)

When one side goes against the enemy with the gods' gift of stronger morale, then their adversaries, as a rule, cannot withstand them.

Willing obedience always beats forced obedience.

Men who think that their officer recognises them are keener to be seen doing something honourable and more desirous of avoiding disgrace.

I am sure that there are young men who can be filled with enthusiasm for serving in the cavalry if one describes the splendour of a cavalryman's life.

Pleasure is what nearly all cavalry training involves. It is the closest a man can get, as far as I know, to flying, and that is something people long to be able to do.

Y

Isoroku Yamamoto

(1884–1943, Japanese naval commander)

I will run wild for six months... after that,
I have no expectation of success.
After the attack on Pearl Harbour in December 1941

A military man can scarcely pride himself on
having 'smitten a sleeping enemy'; it is more a
matter of shame, simply, for the one smitten.

Yamamoto Tsunetomo

(1659–1719, Japanese samurai)

When one has made a decision to kill a person...
it will not do to think about going at it in a long
roundabout way... The way of the Samurai is one
of immediacy, and it is best to dash in headlong.

Z

BAHADUR SHAH ZAFAR

(1775–1862, LAST MUGHAL EMPEROR)

As long as there remains the scent of faith
in the hearts of our Ghazis (warriors), so
long shall the Talwar (sword) of Hindustan
flash before the throne of London.

EMILIANO ZAPATA

(1879–1919, MEXICAN REVOLUTIONARY)

It is better to die upon your feet than
to live upon your knees.

THE RELUCTANT REVOLUTIONARY

BY THE TIME BAHADUR Shah Zafar inherited the Mughal Empire in 1837, it barely stretched further than the walls of the Red Fort that he inhabited in Delhi. The British East India Company controlled the country and he was a mere figurehead. His interests in any event lay in Sufism, to which he was utterly devoted, and in poetry, which he enjoyed writing.

Suddenly, in 1857, he became caught up in the Indian Rebellion that followed the Sepoy mutiny (which had been partly caused by the pre-greased cartridges that the Sepoys had to bite open before loading into their Enfield rifles: if the grease derived from pork, it was offensive to Muslims; if the grease derived from beef, it was offensive to Hindus). The rebels needed a figure that could unite all Indians, Hindu and Muslim alike, until the British could be defeated, and the 'ruling' Mughal emperor fitted the bill perfectly. Bahadur Shah Zafar did what he could, and made all the right speeches, but defeat was not long in coming. He was captured by the British, tried for treason and sent into exile.

Several movies have since depicted his leading role during the rebellion, the first major anti-British movement in India, but it is somewhat ironic that such a pious and poetic man should be thus immortalised as a revolutionary leader, albeit a very brief and reluctant one.

José Luis Rodríguez Zapatero

(BORN 1960, SPANISH PRIME MINISTER)

You can't bomb a people just in case.
Speaking about the war in Iraq

No Spanish government has given in to terror
and no Spanish government will do that.

Mottoes, Maxims and Proverbs

Be the Best
British Army

Si vis pacem, para bellum
(If you wish for peace, prepare for war)
Royal Navy

Per Ardua ad Astra
(Through Adversity to the Stars)
Royal Air Force

Who Dares, Wins
Special Air Service

By Strength and Guile
Special Boat Service

Per Mare, Per Terram
(By Sea, By Land)
Royal Marines

Utrinque Paratus
(Ready for Anything)
Parachute Regiment

Nemo me impune lacessit
(No one assails me with impunity)
Scots Guards

Every Legionnaire is your brother-at-arms,
irrespective of his nationality, race or creed.
You will demonstrate this by an unwavering
and straightforward solidarity that must always
bind together members of the same family.
From the Code of Honour of the French Foreign Legion

Never give a sword to a man who can't dance.
Celtic proverb

If you seek revenge, first prepare two graves.
Chinese proverb

The more you sweat in peacetime,
the less you bleed during war.
Chinese proverb

Fall seven times, stand up eight.
Japanese proverb

Jo bole so nihal, sat sri akal.
(Blessed is the person who recites the
name of God with a true heart.)
Punjabi greeting and Sikh war cry

SIKH REGIMENT,
(BRITISH) INDIAN ARMY

SIKH REGIMENTS HAVE LONG used this Punjabi call to action during battle. Colonel F. T. Birdwood reported one such occasion in his book *The Sikh Regiment in the Second World War*, when he described how the Sikhs galvanised themselves to repel a Japanese advance in the Burmese jungle in 1944. They succeeded. In fact, the Sikhs fought bravely and to great effect on a number of battlefronts across Europe, Asia and North Africa in World War Two. The Sikh Regiment is today one of the most highly decorated regiments in the Indian Army, having previously been one of the most highly decorated regiments in the British Empire. They are not soldiers to be messed with!

Sat sri akal (God is truth) is also used as a more general greeting, shortened nowadays to 'SSA' for the less military purposes of Punjabi SMS text messaging!

The angry man will defeat himself
in battle as well as in life.
Samurai proverb

Take arrows in your forehead, but never in your back.
Samurai proverb

Never walk away from home ahead of
your axe and sword. You can't feel a battle
in your bones or foresee a fight.
From Hávamál (Book of Viking Wisdom)

Lo, there do I see the line of my people
Back to the beginning.
Lo, they do call to me.
They bid me to take my place among them
In the halls of Valhalla!
Where the brave may live forever!
From a Viking war prayer

Always remember to pillage BEFORE you burn.
Viking proverb